Remembering with Love
Messages of Hope
for the First Year of Grieving
and Beyond

Elizabeth Levang, Ph.D.
Sherokee Ilse

FAIRVIEW PRESS
Minneapolis

ISBN: 978-0-925190-86-4

Library of Congress Catalog Number 92-072158

Printed in the United States of America
11 12   16 15 14

Cover design: Circus Design

Dedication

With love
we dedicate this book
to all whose names are memorialized
within these pages
and to those
who honor them.

To the children of my heart, Natalie, Tifanne, and Bryce, and to my gracious husband Curt; thank you for showing me life's possibilities.

—Elizabeth Levang

In memory of my loved ones who have died: Mom, Gram, Gramps, and my children, Brennan, Marama, and Bryna. They live on in my heart forever.

And in special tribute to my beloved husband David and cherished sons, Kellan and Trevor, whose understanding and support allow me the freedom to share of myself.

—Sherokee Ilse

Acknowledgments

We wish to thank all those who willingly bared their souls, sharing their love, sorrow, and memories within the pages of this book. Their lives have now been intertwined with our own, and we have been enriched and enlightened.

We owe thanks as well to:

Jack Caravela, our editor, who was a positive force throughout our project. His wisdom, optimism, and unwavering belief in us proved to be invaluable.

Ed Wedman, our editor-in-chief, whose excitement for our idea and commitment to high standards encouraged us all along the way.

Andrea Gambill, editor of *Bereavement* magazine, for her cooperation and assistance.

Sascha Wagner, for her creative and personal support.

Maggie Merkow, Mary Connell, and Mary Laing Kingston, who served as sounding boards, offering encouragement and insight when they were most needed.

Introduction

Your world may feel like it has suddenly stopped. Sadly, your loved one has died. It's so unfair, and it hurts so much. You weren't ready for this tragedy and you may scarcely know how to go on. It's hard to stop thinking of your loved one. They are your first waking thought and the last thing you think of at night. There is a gaping hole in your life.

While darkness and confusion may surround you, the purpose of *Remembering With Love* is to affirm your feelings and bring you hope to light your path. Having traveled our own journeys of grief, we know how important it is to have a constant source of support. We hope you will keep this book beside you in the days and months to come and use it as you seek the reassurance of knowing you are not alone.

Within this book you will find the voices of many others who have struggled along their own paths, coped, and survived. Their experiences emphasize that every individual has a right to their feelings and ways of coping, and that no matter what others may say, you have the right to grieve for as long and as hard as you need to. It is our hope that their messages, combined with ours, will help you find the courage and strength that are within you.

How to Use This Book

No two people experience grief in precisely the same way, and no one can tell you how to grieve. It is a process that can't be rushed or avoided. There are no simple shortcuts—it must be lived. Our intention is *not* to provide a formula or roadmap to grieving. Instead, we have chosen to include a wide range of feelings, options, issues, and experiences that, hopefully, you will relate to as your grief ebbs and flows over time.

There are nearly three hundred entries within *Remembering With Love*. You may want to start at the beginning and follow along, or use the Reader's Guide to locate the specific topics that coincide with your own needs. Some pages may feel appropriate for a particular day, while others may not. We invite you to draw the messages you find most meaningful into your heart and leave the others for another time. You may also wish to revisit pages that are especially meaningful to you.

This book begins with a section titled *The Early Days*. These pages offer immediate words of encouragement which can be read daily during this trying time.

As the weeks and months progress, new challenges and concerns will confront you. The sections titled *The Early Weeks* and *The Uneven Path* address issues that may surface at this time, allowing you to find the messages that speak to your own concerns.

As you continue your struggle to heal, you may notice that at times your feelings may become less intense. At some point you may discover that you are having more good days than bad, when the pain of grief will not always seem quite so overwhelming. The section titled *The Continuing Journey Towards Healing* helps you recognize your progress toward renewal while continuing to offer validation of your woundedness.

As important as it is to recognize that you have survived the first year, we are aware that grieving does not abruptly end after the first anniversary. The section titled *Beyond The First Year* takes you past this point, offering ongoing emotional support.

Special Days, Moments, and Concerns is a collection of poetry and prose for birthdays, anniversaries, holidays, and considerations of particular significance. You may find a need for additional encouragement at these critical times.

Finally, a resource list of support organizations is included at the end of this book for your use. We hope it will help you find additional sources of strength during this most difficult and trying journey.

*Our heartfelt wish is that by immersing yourself within these pages you will gather these messages of hope to your heart and your soul, so that you can live the rest of your life **Remembering with Love**.*

—Elizabeth Levang and Sherokee Ilse

Reader's Guide

The Early Days

A Death Has Occurred
by Paul Irion

A death has occurred and everything is changed.
We are painfully aware
that life can never be the same again,
that yesterday is over,
that relationships once rich have ended.
But there is another way to look upon this truth.
If life now went on the same,
without the presence of the one who has died,
we could only conclude that the life we remember
made no contribution, filled no space, meant nothing.
The fact that this person left behind a place
that cannot be filled
is a high tribute to this individual.
Life can be the same after a trinket has been lost,
but never after the loss of a treasure.

Feeling Unprepared

"I always knew
He would die
But not this year
Not this season
This month
This week
This day
This hour
This moment—
Not now"
     Ellen Olinger, in memory of her father,
Harold A. Borgh.

     We all know that death is an inevitable part of living. Yet when our loved one dies, we can scarcely comprehend the timing. "Why did she have to die *now?*" questions a distraught family member. It does not matter if death came slowly or suddenly; it all seems so unbelievable. We feel unprepared. But do we really think that another time would be better, or less painful? No. It is unlikely we can ever be ready. There can be no right time.

It is a struggle to accept that my loved one has died at this particular moment in my life. Though I feel unprepared, I can acknowledge that no time would have been the right time.

Unnaturalness of Funeral Rites

"In death, my brother's face was not the one I knew. It seemed so fake, so made up. 'Could this be a dream?' I thought. The entire funeral was strange—family, friends, even enemies were there. It was the worst day of my life."

Michelle Dubreuil, in loving memory of her brother, Rich.

Reviewal rites and funeral services can have an unreal or dreamlike quality about them. Seeing our loved one so still and peaceful can feel unnatural and confusing. We may look for a flutter of the eyelid, or the grin we are so used to seeing. What we have known of our loved one may not correspond with what we see at this moment.

Few of us are familiar with death. Seeing our loved one in this way is not natural to us. However, we can accept that there are no right feelings at this time, nor rules about how we are to react at services. It is best not to place high demands on ourselves. Crying, being numb, or feeling confused are all acceptable.

I will not place unrealistic expectations on myself. I can accept that at this time there are no rules about proper feelings. Feeling confused, strange, or dazed is okay.

Numbness

"It is as if a darkness blankets my feelings. I am numb to the world."

   Dan Laik, in memory of a special friend.

At times our emotions may become so intense, so overpowering, that we begin to feel as if we are numb, out of touch with everyone and everything around us. The numbness may feel like a heavy, dark cloth that blankets all emotions. It may cover the raw feelings that assault us and momentarily soothe our confusion and pain. That numbness is a sign for us to rest—physically, mentally, and emotionally.

It is okay to feel numb. I will temporarily give way to this numbness and let it give me time to revive and renew myself. I can rest.

Comfort in Mourning

"Everyone told me to be strong, that she wouldn't want to see me so upset. But I believe that by mourning for my mother I was expressing my love for her. I know she wouldn't mind my tears; they were a gift of love."

Janice Hewett, in loving memory of her mother, Marcia Wood.

By being able to mourn we demonstrate our great love. We miss our loved one and need to express our sorrow. It is a great tribute to them that we care so much. Mourning can bring comfort as we reexperience the life of our loved one and the impact it had on us.

As hard as it may be to realize at times, to be able to mourn for someone really is a gift—to them and to ourselves. This painful process allows us to move our feelings from inside of us to the outside, to share them with others, to remember the love, life, and dreams that sprang from our loved one's specialness.

Today I will look at mourning as a gift of love, a tribute to my loved one.

Taking Care of Ourselves

"After mother died, we asked our six year old daughter how she felt. She said, 'It feels like I have a flat tire in my stomach.'"

> Ken and Regina Pugh, in loving memory of Ken's mother.

The shock of our loved one's death does affect us physically. Like Ken and Regina's daughter, many of us have that sinking feeling in the pit of our stomach. It's as if we can barely muster enough air to keep going. We may feel faint and weak all over.

The heaviness and achiness we feel are a normal part of grieving. Yet we must be careful not to let these physical ailments take a toll on our body. It's important to take care of ourselves, getting plenty of rest and eating regularly. A short walk, or some other exercise can also be of help.

The achiness and physical discomforts I have are a part of grieving. I will take care of myself today. I will eat, rest, and get a bit of exercise.

Anger with God

"Why did this happen? It's so unfair. Why me? Why now? I'm so angry that God let this happen."
Anonymous

When faced with a loved one's death, it is quite natural to begin to question why. A sorrowful son may cry out, "It's not fair that Dad is dead."

"Why did God have to take my beautiful daughter?" lashes out a grieving mother.

At this time, no matter what our faith, it may be particularly easy to be truly angry with God. Since He isn't physically here to provide ready replies, He becomes a target for our unanswered suffering.

We may question God's mercy or justice and demand that He answer our questions. In our anger, we may turn away from God, feeling that because He abandoned us or brought pain into our lives, we have no need for Him.

Anger is sometimes a dark, scary emotion. Though we may not feel that it is right to be angry with God, it is helpful to believe that anger is okay, even when it is directed at God.

Without holding back, I will tell God that I am angry with Him. I can find a moment of quiet solitude and share my feelings of frustration, disappointment, and despair with Him.

Grieving is Natural

"Grieving is as natural as crying when you are hurt,
sleeping when you are tired,
eating when you are hungry,
or sneezing when your nose itches.
It is nature's way of healing a broken heart."
      *from **Don't Take My Grief Away**, by Reverend*
Doug Manning.

     Grief and sorrow are frightening to many people. We don't know what to expect. We may fear that if we allow ourselves to hurt so much, we will die. Grief can seem like such an unnatural process, much like an uncontrollable disease.

     Yet, as Doug writes, grief is actually the most natural response when we are deeply hurt. Grief is nature's, or God's, way of healing a broken heart. We should not be afraid of it, or try to avoid it. Rather, we can look at this painful journey as a way to tell us, and the world, how much we love and will miss our special one.

I will not fear the grief and sorrow that now encompass me. I can make this healing journey with the will to survive.

Sharing Our Tears With Others

"Friends who came to visit after my husband's sudden death apologized for bringing tears to my eyes, but how very necessary and soothing those tears were. The tight, hard knot of pain was smoothed and eased by the shared tearful moments."

Betty Wolner, in loving memory of her first husband, Harvey.

Our society offers no 'practical' education in the experience of grieving and mourning. Our family, friends, and co-workers may be afraid of our pain, our tears, and our sorrow. They may avoid the sensitive questions or comments, hoping to keep us from crying. They may search for ways to help us, often believing that well-meaning advice is what we need. Yet the very things we may need the most are their presence and their support in helping us to express our feelings.

The tension and pain we hold inside needs to find its release. Shedding tears is not a sign of weakness, as many think, or something to be afraid of. Rather, it may be what strengthens us. We may need to let others know that we do not want them to avoid the closeness that may bring tears. When they help open the floodgates and we cry in their presence, they may be giving us one of the greatest gifts of all.

I will not be afraid of shedding tears in front of others. I will remember that tears can ease my pain.

Details and Decision Making

"So many details to see to, so many decisions to make and people to face. The rollercoaster of emotions never stopped its relentless ride, but the deepest loneliness of grief could be held at bay—for a time—when there were clothes to buy, rituals to plan and other people at hand."

*from **Parting is not Goodbye**, by Kelly Osmont, in loving memory of her son, Aaron, who died at age nineteen from a horse accident.*

The details, decisions, and confusion during the first few weeks after a death can be overwhelming. On top of that, our emotions are often uncontrollable. Thankfully, shock and numbness may cushion us to a degree. But that often lasts for only a short time, and then it's easy to be overcome by anguish and loneliness.

Surviving these intense times may mean pouring ourselves into planning the service, surrounding ourselves with people, and keeping busy with details. This coping style may be necessary to get certain tasks accomplished, like arranging the funeral and settling the estate. Staying occupied can also become a way to keep our loneliness and deep emotions at bay. If this is helpful to us, we need to recognize that it's okay to stay busy with details.

I will admit to myself that it is okay to get caught up in the details of what I must do at this time. Today I can allow these tasks to temporarily fill the void and keep my emotions at bay, if I need to.

The Early Days

Well-Meaning Friends

"Friends cleaned my house, took everything I had in my daughters' room except their cribs, and put it all away. It made me mad. I felt they were taking away what little bit I had left."

> *Cara Duffey, in memory of her twins, Kara and Kayla.*

Our family and friends want to help us in any way they can. They care for us and want to ease our pain. In an attempt to help, they may decide to get rid of the painful possessions that might be reminders of our loved one, or pressure us to take care of this task right away. However, this is a decision which we must make for ourselves.

If we are distressed because people have made inappropriate decisions for us or given us unhelpful advice, we can consider sharing our feelings with them. We can let them know that while we appreciate their good intentions, they are not being helpful. We can tell them what we might have preferred.

I have a right to my feelings when decisions are made or advice given that isn't helpful to me. When possible, I will ask others to give me the freedom to make my own decisions.

Snatched Away

"Those first few mornings after Kevin died were so difficult. To wake up and have it all come back at you— not being able to hold him, love him, or take care of him would start the tears flowing. All of our hopes, dreams, and plans for him that could not be realized... At times it was overwhelming."

> Dolores Menz, in loving memory of her son, Kevin, who died five days after birth.

The first days after a loved one dies can be shocking and overwhelming. We may feel as if they were snatched away from us, even if we had a chance to say goodbye. They are supposed to be in our life, near us, available to us. We may turn a corner expecting to see or talk with them, only to suddenly remember they are gone. It can be so unbelievable.

We may have a deep desire to turn the clock back. How could this tragedy have suddenly happened to us, to our loved one? It seems so unreal. They should be here, yet they are not. The pain of their absence mounts as sadness and shock assault us. Yet, we still have our dreams and our memories. In time they will bring us comfort.

It is hard to believe that my loved one was snatched away. Much as I would like, however, I cannot turn back the clock. Today I can look for a touch of sunlight in my path.

Lack of Concentration

"I started to make lists of things I had to do. I just couldn't concentrate long enough to get anything done, I felt so preoccupied. I felt like I was on automatic pilot."

Juliana Ehrman, in memory of her grandmother, Katherine Immel.

We may be overloaded emotionally, spiritually, and intellectually by our loved one's death. Quite naturally, we may have trouble hearing, making decisions, and concentrating. We may feel bewildered and easily confused. It's as if we are on automatic pilot.

We may find comfort by reassuring ourselves that this condition is temporary. It is one of the effects of our heavy grieving and our preoccupation with our loved one's death. We will not stay this way forever.

To deal with the difficulties we are having remembering and concentrating, we may want to make lists, checking things off when they are done. If we need to make a decision or complete a task that requires close attention, we may want to ask someone to assist us or put it off for just awhile. For the time being, we may need to do things a little differently.

If I forget something or become easily confused I will allow myself to be human by forgiving myself, then letting it go. If it helps, I will use lists for awhile to aid my memory and concentration.

Calmness from Walking

"During the hard days of grieving, as well as the less intense days that followed, I would take many walks, to be by myself and to reminisce. They always seemed to refresh and calm me, as I recalled my loved one's influence on my life."

Pat Barker, in loving memory of her mother, Margaret Grey, and her grandmother, Bertha Woodard.

Something so simple as walking may surprise us in its power to calm and refresh us. The adrenaline pumps through our body, our heart beats faster, and our emotions can be refreshed from the exercise of a brisk walk. Or, a slow and peaceful walk can help calm us, even if just for the time being. We may also find walking to be an opportunity to relive the influence our loved one has had on our family's lives.

When we walk, we can try to keep our heads up high, our bodies straight, and our thoughts open to the moment. We may find this activity quickly becoming a habit—our daily pick-me-up.

I can use walking to help me gain peace, solitude, and a respite from my daily problems and issues. I will let my walk revitalize my mind and body.

Religious Traditions and
the Need to Grieve

"At my Uncle Dan's funeral, the minister said we should be happy that Dan is now with his Savior. He told us that Heaven is more important than this earthly life. His words were hard to swallow. I felt like he was telling me I should stop grieving."

Anonymous

Some faiths see death as a time of triumphant rejoicing, as it signifies our loved one's arrival at their eternal home. Our interpretation may be that we should deny our sorrow and be filled with joy, for our loved one has now reached a most glorious place.

It may be comforting to think about the one we love being in a better place. Still, we cannot deny our need to grieve. It's important for us not to feel we are devaluing our loved one's earthly existence and the unique mark they made in this life by suppressing our tears. Thoughts of eternal life alone cannot end our grief.

I can be grateful and happy that my loved one has reached the safety of their eternal home and is at peace. At the same time, I can grieve their passing from my life.

Comfort in Small Accomplishments

"While my wife and mother-in-law put away the crib and baby things after my son died, my father-in-law and I split wood. His arm on my shoulder, his sober face of shared concern, and later a stack of wood—something accomplished—all helped me feel sane at an insane time."

David Ilse, in loving memory of his son, Brennan.

There are many ways of expressing and sharing grief. Whether we paint, work on a project, prepare a meal, or build something, either by ourselves or standing shoulder to shoulder with others, the normalcy of routine chores can help to bring comfort during these troubling times. We do not need to talk or "process" all of our pain and grief in order to give and receive support. Doing something may give us a sense of escape and hope for the moment, and it may be a way for others to show that they care. Their silent support may be all we need right now.

I can find ways to help me feel better other than talking about my loss. I can accomplish one small thing today, either by myself or with someone working beside me.

Am I Going Crazy?

"There have been times in my grief when I thought I was losing my mind, and other times I was sure it was already gone."

Linda Taylor Williams, in loving memory of her husband.

The mixture of feelings that accompanies grief often has us thinking we're going crazy. We may be anxious, nervous, panic-stricken, confused, and uncertain. Our thoughts may be jumbled and our life out of control.

The sense of losing our sanity is a dizzying experience. It can distort our sense of self, and we may feel worthless and incompetent. Our grief is slowly wearing us down.

For now, it may be helpful to realize that our feelings are all very normal. We are undergoing a tremendous amount of stress, and feeling that we're losing control of our mental faculties is a natural outcome. Getting plenty of rest, fluids, exercise, and eating well can give us the confidence and strength we need to eventually feel in control again.

At times, the stress of my grief has me feeling crazy. I will work to restore my self-worth and strength by resting, exercising, and eating well.

Going Back to Work

"I knew returning to work would be very hard, not only for me, but also for everyone I worked with. I sent them a group card thanking them for the support they'd shown me, and told them it was okay to talk to me about my miscarriage. I knew I had to give them permission and the tools to make my returning easier."

Kyle Bemboom

Returning to work after the death of a loved one may be something we look forward to so we can stay busy, or we may dread it. Performing up to standards may be one worry, and facing our co-workers may be an even bigger one. Like Kyle, we may want to find a way to ease back into the workplace.

It might be helpful to have a talk with our boss, explaining our emotional and physical condition and asking for understanding. We also may want to talk with co-workers about our needs and wishes. Some of us may be able to do this directly, while others may find a note or letter easier.

If going back to work is hard for me, I can actively do something to make the transition easier for both me and my co-workers.

Fear of Haunting Memories

"My father died a tortuous death in an intensive care unit (ICU). In the last 48 hours of his life he was almost unrecognizable. I was so afraid that those memories would haunt me forever. Thankfully, a good friend who had been an ICU nurse for years told me that I had 28 years of 'well' memories, and to trust that eventually those well images would take over my memory. At the time I was having nightmares, and really wanted to believe her. She was right; within six months the memories of my father's final days began to fade."

Donna Damico Mayer, in memory of her father, Joseph Damico.

We may fear that the sight of our loved one suffering near the end of their life, or in the casket at the funeral, will become a lasting memory that stays with us over time. Although this does not usually happen, the fear is real.

It is natural for these memories to haunt us for awhile, finding their way into our dreams or thoughts in the days that follow. We may still be having trouble integrating our loss into our reality, and the freshness of the agony can overwhelm and consume us. But over time, these haunting memories will fade; we can trust in this. We can help the process along by looking at pictures from happier times, sharing stories of our loved one's life with others, or turning our minds to pleasant memories.

If my memories of my loved one haunt me, I will remind myself that they are temporary. When possible, I will recall the happy, "well" memories. I trust that these will be my lasting memories.

Coping Through Prayer

"While mom was dying and even after she died, I began to pray more often than I normally did. In my prayers I asked God for strength for me and my family. I felt like I couldn't go through mom's death alone. My prayers brought me inner strength."

Monica Nelson, in loving memory of her mother, Creta Mullenmaster.

For those of us who have faith in the healing power of God, great consolation can come to us through prayer. Like food for the heart and soul, prayer is a way of strengthening and fortifying us during the long famine of our grief.

For many of us, survival during these desolate times is dependent on the sustaining nourishment we receive from our prayers. Praying is a way of coping with our trauma; it allows us to move outside our pain and seek relief in a source larger than ourself.

One of the ways I can cope with my pain is to seek the nourishment that comes from praying. Today I will ask God to be with me and give me strength.

The Right To Grieve

"I felt in such an awkward position after my uncle died. I was not the central person affected by his death; my aunt was. Yet I felt a tremendous sense of loss. Did I have the right to grieve his death too?"

> Elizabeth Levang, in loving memory of her uncle, Tony Rizzo.

When a loved one dies, we naturally think about the grieving partner, children, or parents. Still, other family members and even close friends may be deeply affected. We cared and loved for them; how can we not grieve?

We all have a right to our grief. There are no limits or conditions on who can grieve. Our feelings are our own and no one can take them away. It does not matter how long we have known this special person, nor our position in the family circle.

I have a right to my grief. All that matters is that I cared for this special person, and that I miss them.

Difficulties Settling The Estate

"Shortly after my dad's funeral I went to his house to go over his personal belongings, and I found that a number of special things were missing. My sister had already been there. It felt like something had been lost, and I was very hurt. I didn't talk to my sister for a very long time and never saw her again. I finally let go and forgave her. I went to visit her one year only to learn she had recently died."

Keith Parks, in loving memory of his parents, Cecil and Emily, and his sister, Melba.

Sometimes, settling our loved one's estate can lead to misunderstandings, hurt feelings, or even a division in the family. Deciding about belongings is difficult, and making decisions that are agreeable to everyone can be a challenge.

Looking back, we can often see the huge strain we were under and realize that we were not our normal selves at the time. All the demands on us may have made us especially sensitive and, feeling on edge, some of us may have been unreasonable or stubborn, even though we never intended to be.

Admittedly, our loved one's death was a painful time, and emotions may have flared up more easily under the strain. We may need to forgive ourselves and our family. Family is important; being angry and resentful does not help our grieving, and in the long run these feelings may prove damaging.

If a loving relationship with my family has been jeopardized, I will do my best to mend it. Family is important to me. I will attempt to let go of my resentments and anger.

The Early Days

Accepting Helpful Support

"Accepting the love, kindnesses, and generosity of others was very important. Opening my heart to the many kindnesses offered to us brought both healing tears of thankfulness and a lessening of loneliness."

Betty Wolner, in loving memory of her first husband.

Family and friends can be a key to survival at our time of loss, as well as in the weeks and months that follow. During the lonely and difficult times, we are reminded how important our relationships are. Friends and acquaintances may send cards, flowers, prepare meals, or offer some other kindness. The outpouring of love and concern is very meaningful to us. Though thankful that we are blessed with such special, caring friends, it may not always be easy to accept help.

It may be surprising, but this can be a time when new relationships begin. We may find an entire new network of support that we never had before. Support may come from people who have had similar losses, from our faith, community, and even from people we don't know very well who offer to share their compassion with us.

I will accept help and support from others. Their love and concern may lessen my loneliness and bring healing, which I truly need right now.

Seeking Closeness Through Nature

"I planted a tree honoring my daughter. As her tree grows tall and healthy I feel connected to her tree and to her. I call it Marion's tree. And even though her little hand will never touch that tree, I know it has been touched by her heart and that is enough for me."

Alice Rademacher, in memory of her daughter, Marion Marie.

We all have times when we seek a closeness with our loved ones who have died. There are many ways to do this: by remembering them, speaking to their spirit within us, or doing something symbolic to honor them. The planting of a tree, or flowers is a special way to experience life while honoring our loved one. We can watch the changes of a tree or a flower and feel their presence through the natural wonder of life.

I can find closeness with my loved one through nature and its beauty.

The Changing Nature of Grief

"When grief is new, it wraps your life in pain.
When grief goes on, it teaches you endurance.
When grief grows up, it shows you how to heal."
    sascha, in loving memory of Eve and
Nino Hendee, her splendid children.

Grief can be intimidating and frightening. At first the pain of grief overwhelms us. We wonder if we will be able to survive, and we may have trouble sleeping, thinking clearly, and even functioning on a basic level. As sascha tells us, new grief seems to wrap itself around our being. We may fear we are being smothered, and yet we can feel so very alone. It is as if time has stopped; life is on hold.

As hard as it may be to imagine, grief changes as it continues on, taking a variety of new forms. In time, grief challenges us to survive, to keep loving and remembering in spite of the pain. Hopefully, we will find others to share our stories with, and to offer us support. This can help us endure.

When grief grows up, we still feel some pain, but there is some joy present, too. We may feel proud of how we have coped and survived. We may notice ways we have changed and ways we have grown.

Grief is no easy journey. In fact, it is a very strenuous struggle that affects us deeply as we remember, love, and heal.

Even though my grief may be new and extremely painful, I will take a moment to recognize this journey as one of love. It will be a changing process and will not always be so painful or intense.

Rage

"Anger comes silently.
I am overcome by a painful rage...

Must I submit to the rage
in order to be
at peace with myself?"
      *from **The Anguish of Loss** by Julie Fritsch, in*
loving memory of Justin.

The anger we feel at the time of our loss and in the days that follow may frighten us. We may wonder what we can do with such violent rage. Often it's difficult even to know whom we are angry with. This general outcry of anger and unfairness can be directed at no one and everyone.

Many of us are uncomfortable expressing anger, or afraid of hurting ourselves or others by letting it out. We often believe that if we keep it inside and pretend we are fine, it will simply go away. Yet anger turned inward often grows.

Anger can get in the way of moving on and through the mourning process. One way to work towards peace and healing is to express our anger in constructive ways. Some of us may find it helpful to exercise, pound our fists on pillows, or write a letter to those we are angry with, even if we don't intend to send it.

I can submit to my rage, my anger, without hurting myself or others. I have a right to my anger and I will find a safe and constructive way to express it.

Dwelling on Our Loved One's Death

"My mind reruns Alexander's death start to finish. Like a movie, I see each part replayed again and again. Each segment presents itself for me to analyze, to pick apart, to reconcile in my mind. The shock is so profound that I have to relive it a thousand times over until I can convince myself that it is real."

Joanetta Hendel, in memory of her son, Alexander.

Like Joanetta, many of us go over and over the details of our loved one's death time after agonizing time. The days, hours, and minutes preceding their death become a kind of mental movie that replays itself endlessly. Though it is painful, reliving each incident and moment slowly helps to convince us of what is true. We cannot change what has happened. Each time we reexperience our loss we come a little closer to accepting our loved one's death.

Replaying the events of my loved one's death eases my shock and helps me believe that they are gone. The devastation I feel needs time to heal.

Sexuality

"I feel like I buried my sexuality with my loved one."
Anonymous

It may take some time before we have any desire to be intimate or have sex again. That part of our life may appear to have closed down, at least for now. Many of us may not feel particularly feminine or masculine. We may not be as content with ourselves as we would wish.

Ours has been a terrible ordeal. Normal activities and routines have been disturbed and, in many ways, we may feel disoriented and out of step with life. Being sexual may be the furthest thing from our mind.

We need to give ourselves permission to accept our level of sexual needs. This aspect of our life needs to heal as well, and pressuring ourselves or feeling guilty is not helpful.

I can decide when it's right for me to be sexual or intimate again. I will not heap guilt or pressure on myself. I will let this part of my life heal.

Intimacy and Support

"Why is it so hard for people to touch a grieving person? Don't people know that we crave their hugs more than their words?"

   C. Renee Anderson, in loving memory of her husband, Keith.

As we grieve the loss of our loved one, we may sense that others are uncomfortable with grief. Most people have had such little experience with death that they're not sure how to show support. They may fumble for the right words, and maybe stroke our hands or pat us on the shoulder, but beyond these actions, few know how to extend intimacy to a grieving person. While talk can be helpful, hugs of genuine support and understanding feel like a warm blanket of love around us.

We can have compassion for those who are not sure how to support a grieving person. Strong, supportive relationships are important to us during this time. We can show our friends and family how to be with us and, hopefully, in the process we will gain the intimacy and support we need.

I can help those who want to support me but just don't know how. I can teach my friends and family what my needs are.

My Life Stops, But The World Goes On

"Life is never the same after one experiences the death of a loved one. Initially, it's impossible to understand how the world can continue to go on as if nothing monumental has happened—don't they know that a special person has died?"

Dr. Beverly Musgrave, in memory of her parents, Mr. & Mrs. Fred P. Musgrave.

Our life, our world, has suddenly stopped. Yet we often are expected to continue about our daily lives as if the death of our loved one is only a minor setback. Most of us are expected to return to work, or to other responsibilities within days or weeks. We are told that we should be alert, attentive, and working at our full capacity. For many of us, the thought of going about the business of life feels unrealistic; we can scarcely stop thinking about our loved one, and we struggle to put one foot in front of the other!

There is no rigid timetable that dictates when we should go back to work, or when we can handle more than routine responsibilities. Our world has changed; it will never be the same. If those around us seem insensitive or lack understanding, we must not be afraid to help them understand how we feel.

The world has stopped for me. I will seek ways to adapt to this changed world.

Alone With Our Pain

"The absolute worst day after my father died came about four weeks after his death. It was the first day that no one called and there were no letters in the mail. I knew then that I was alone with my pain."

   Donna Damico Mayer, in loving memory of her father, Joseph Damico.

For most of us, the day eventually comes when no one is there to support us. On this day we feel so very alone; the calls, visitors, and cards have stopped coming. It may happen after a few weeks or months after our loved one's death. Friends and family go back to their busy lives, hoping that we can do the same. They may be thinking that it's not good for us to dwell on this too long; they want us to move on.

On days when we feel so alone, we may wonder if it's time to put our grief behind us. Are we grieving too long? Have we worn our friends out? While these questions are normal, we need to remember that others cannot determine the appropriate length of our grief. We can trust ourselves; we are the best judges of our own needs.

If I feel alone with my grief today because I have less support, I will do something special for myself. I can call a close friend or relative and tell them I need a shoulder to lean on today.

Healing Through Humor

*"I believe that each of us will find the laughter that echoed throughout our life with our loved one...if we will look for it. We all deserve to be happy again. It's a different kind of happy, however. It's a happiness robbed of innocence, born out of fire, forged by a flame that has the power to destroy everything in its path-but **only if we let it!**"*

Darcie Sims, in loving memory of her son, Austin, who died after a lifelong battle with a malignant brain tumor.

Finding the humor that once occupied our lives may be one of the hardest tasks we face in our grief. Many of us feel guilty for even thinking of laughing. "How could anything be funny?" we wonder. Humorous incidents are hastily dismissed. Grieving people don't laugh, do they?

In reality, humor has been found to aid survival and healing. When we laugh we release endorphins, the body's natural painkiller. Endorphins have a calming and relaxing effect on our body. They help us slow down and momentarily forget about our pain.

Darcie is right; we all deserve to be happy again. A little humor may bring that touch of sunshine we need and help us heal just a bit faster.

I want to be happy again, someday. Now and then, I will let a little laughter help cheer me and make the day more bearable.

Repetition and Preoccupation

"I would catch myself saying the same thing over and over. I remember telling a friend at least three times in the same conversation about a card my sister had sent me. It got to be terribly embarrassing. I could hardly concentrate anymore and I felt so worn out and tired."

Tracey Legge, in memory of her dad, Everett Schwartzkopf.

Many of us find ourselves repeating the same things again and again. It's as if our memory isn't quite working, and our thinking isn't so clear. We have trouble recalling what we've just uttered, and so we repeat the same story or event over and over. Not only might we be embarrassed, but we might often feel exhausted from trying to concentrate and keep our thoughts straight.

This repetition can be a result of preoccupation. Our mind may be so engaged with thoughts of our loved one that we scarcely have time to consider other matters, let alone remember them. As time passes and thoughts of our loved one are less constant, our minds can return to other things. We will find it easier to concentrate and remember without repeating ourselves.

I can repeat myself without feeling embarrassed. My loved one's death has been a tremendous shock and, for now, I may be preoccupied with thoughts about them. I will take time to rest and renew myself so I don't feel quite so exhausted.

Peace

"Yes, I feel robbed, cheated, and hurt, but I am comforted in the knowledge that they are safe and warm in heaven."
        Cara Duffey, in memory of her twins, Kara and Kayla.

For those who believe in heaven or an afterlife, solace may be found in the conviction that our loved one is safe and warm in a peaceful, loving place, that they feel no pain and are free from worry. While feelings of sadness, sorrow, and a sense of loneliness still exist, thoughts of our loved one at peace may bring us comfort.

I will seek comfort through peaceful thoughts about my loved one.

Silence Brings Us Back to Reality

"Mom died quietly in the hospital bed she had occupied for several days. Thankfully, I was at her side. When I went back to the house, the home of my childhood, I felt overwhelmed by the silence. Where was Mom? I did not know this home without her! The silence was unbearable."

Leah Jones, in loving memory of her mother and best friend, Ruth.

The absence of our loved one creates a painful and overwhelming silence. We hunger for the very sound of them, yet, our ears reverberate with nothingness, and we strain to retrieve some small remnant of their existence. At times our mind momentarily tricks us into thinking they are still near. Then reality hurdles back, reminding us that they are no longer here. We cannot hear or see them; they are gone. Yet, memories remain.

There is a silence created by my loved one's death. The reality is that they are gone. I can rely on my memories to make reality more bearable.

Violent Pain

"In a violent rush, a savage pain attacked, wounding my throat, my chest, my stomach. Wracking sobs followed the onslaught. I felt a kinship with mourning women who tear their hair and shriek in anguish. Inwardly, that's what I was doing as streams of tears spilled down my cheeks."

from ***Parting is not Goodbye*** by Kelly Osmont, in loving memory of her son, Aaron.

The anguish and despair we feel when a loved one dies can hardly be described. We may feel we cannot stop the savage pain that assaults our body and soul. Our heart and mind may be screaming, even when we look calm or distant on the outside. We share these feelings with families throughout the ages who have grieved and mourned as if their souls were on fire.

We may feel it is irrational to have such intense emotions. But no matter the type of loss, this depth of despair is natural when we have loved someone so deeply. The violent pain can easily overwhelm us, making it difficult to function. We may even wonder if we will live through it, and we may fear for our sanity. Yet, hearing someone else admit to these feelings usually helps us. Once they are affirmed, we may be able to accept our feelings as normal, allowing them to come and go as they will.

My intense feelings of pain and sadness are the outcry of my feelings of love for this special person. I am not alone; others share these same feelings. They are natural.

The Early Weeks

from **Don't Take My Grief Away**
by Reverend Doug Manning

Grief is not an enemy; it is a friend.
It is a natural process of walking through the pain and
growing because of the walk.
Stand up tall to friends and to yourself and say,
　"Don't take my grief away from me.
　I deserve it, and I'm going to have it."

Love Finds a Way

"My husband's sister called late at night from Iran. His mother was dying, slipping in and out of a coma. Five of her children were here in America. I watched and ached, helpless, thoughts of support haunting me: support, foundations, bridges, building blocks, stones... Then the idea struck me. Instructions were wired to find a beautiful smooth stone for each missing member of the family and place them in mother's hand one at a time. A family member's name was repeated as her fingers were pressed around each stone.

"Mother caught on quickly, and as she slept she held a stone in each hand. When conscious, she held conversations with the person whose stone she held, or whispered a message to be given to them. Mother died with the smooth stones in her hands, secure in the knowledge that all her loved ones were with her. The stones were placed in the grave with her.

"While our family was separated, love found a way."
Lila "Peggy" Azad, Ph.D.

Being unable to share our loved one's last days or moments is terribly agonizing. We want to be with them, to support and help them. The distance and circumstances only intensify our anguish. We want them to know of our love.

If we too were unable to be with our loved one, we can let a smooth stone speak for us and convey our love. We can find a special stone or other object to place at the gravesite or at a place of importance that we shared. In this way, we will let our love be known and keep this message in our hearts forever.

In spite of all that has happened, I can let my loved one know how deeply I cared. My love will find a way to carry the message through to eternity.

Emotionally Withdrawing from Others

"When my two and a half year old son died, every ounce of my being protested. 'I didn't ask for this!,' I screamed. My initial reaction was to withdraw from the world around me, a world that I could no longer trust. To protect myself from further hurt and harm, I emotionally distanced myself from my other children, from my family and from my friends."

Joanetta Hendel, in loving memory of her precious little Alexander.

The death of a loved one can cause us to retreat from the world. We may be afraid of being hurt again, but we're doubtful that we can go on alone. The sense of being a failure haunts us like a bad dream. Purposefully or not, we may reject those around us in order to protect our fragile selves.

Turning away from those who love us only lessens the support and protection we badly need. The safety we long for can only come by allowing others to comfort and care for us. We must risk in order to gain trust again.

I will not intentionally drive away those who love me. I will risk letting my family and friends care for me, as I need them to survive and help me trust again.

Creating Memories

"They are all gone into the world of light!
And I alone sit lingering here;
Their very memory is fair and bright,
And my sad thoughts doth clear."
    from **The World, They Are All Gone,** by Henry
Vaughan.

It has been said that our memories are our most
important possessions, for they are all that we truly own.
Unlike other possessions, we constantly carry our memories with us; no one can take them away. These enduring
marks are comprised of the many people, places, events,
and situations which have shaped our lives.

Building and creating memories of our loved one is
an important task. Making a scrapbook of their life,
keeping sympathy cards, preserving flowers, saving
special possessions, or searching deep in our hearts for
buried recollections are all ways to create memories of
the one we loved. These memories give us the strength
we need to survive. They are the vital link with our past
and the fuel for our future. It is important to build
memories with care.

My memories are important reminders of who I
am and those I love. I am my memories. As I face
the day, I will hold tight to these most precious
treasures.

Blaming God

"I was so angry. Nine miscarriages. Whose fault was this? Was it God's fault? I didn't know, but I blamed Him."

   Kyle Bemboom

Many of us spend a great deal of time trying to understand why our loved one died. Finding fault is a common reaction and, sometimes, God becomes an object of our blame. We may feel that with His omnipotent power and ability to work miracles He could have prevented this death, but He didn't. Blaming God may be an agonizing experience because we want to rely on His comfort, yet we feel confused over his role in our loved one's death.

We may never have a complete understanding of all those events which caused our loved one to lose their life, and blaming God can be a natural response as we attempt to make sense of things.

Sometimes there appears to be little sense in what has happened. I realize that blaming God or others won't bring my loved one back or give me all the answers I want.

Difficulty Making Decisions

"Thirty years we had been married. How was I going to go on without him? The mere thought that now I had to take the reins in my own hands was frightening. There were papers to sign and read, bills began to pile up, finances and business matters to take care of. Decisions, decisions, everywhere."

Meg Hale, in memory of her husband.

Once those first traumatic days are behind us, life presents us with even more decisions. There is the will and estate, medical expenses, bills from the funeral, issues around relationships, and other things which may have to be decided. Most of us also face the excruciating decision of how to store or give away our loved one's possessions.

These decisions can weigh heavily on many of us. Decision making may not be our strength, or we may feel afraid or unwilling to take the responsibility just yet. Asking a trusted friend or family member for advice may be helpful for some of us, but we can't forget that their suggestions are just that: suggestions. Ultimately, only we know what is right for us. We must give ourselves the time we need to think and plan carefully, not only for today, but for the future as well.

I am capable of making decisions. I do not have to fear choices. If I want, I can ask for help to gather more information or get another perspective.

The Stages of Grief

"The funeral was over. Was I in shock? At the moment I felt calm, but a rush of pain could hit me any time. It didn't feel like the first in an orderly progression of stages. I'd read about the commonly accepted 'stages of grief,' but I seemed to be a bundle of confusing, scattered emotions that varied hourly."

*from **Parting is not Goodbye** by Kelly Osmont, in loving memory of her son, Aaron.*

Weeks after our loved one's death we are left to wonder what comes next. At times our senses are dull and our feelings empty. This shock is the beginning of grieving. We may hear about denial, bargaining, and other commonly discussed phases of grief, and we may latch onto them as a pattern on which to base our hope. Since the pain is so intense, most of us want a roadmap for healing quickly.

While there are common themes and feelings in grief, the mourning process is unique for everyone. There is no clear roadmap to follow, and grief has its own timetable. Survivors follow their own paths, although their journeys are partially understood by all who have traveled before them.

We may find ourselves angry one minute, unfeeling and numb the next. We may wake up in tears, experience calmness during the afternoon, then find ourselves intensely upset by evening. The lack of control over our emotions can be frightening, but we *can* make it through this long journey. It helps to trust that our scattered and varied emotions are a natural part of grieving.

I will allow myself to experience the roller coaster of feelings that accompany my grief. I will remind myself that while there is no roadmap to clearly point my way, others have traveled a similar path.

Using Visualization To Escape Pain

"There were many days and nights when I couldn't relax or fall asleep after my mother died. I kept seeing her in pain or lying in the casket. I hurt so much—I would sob and sob. The only way I found peace was to picture myself on my favorite beach in Hawaii, listening to the waves and being warmed by the sun."

Sherokee Ilse, in loving memory of her mother, Darlene Parks.

Finding peace and a sense of calmness may be difficult for us now. But we can find solace, if just for a short while, by imagining ourselves in a relaxing, restful place. By immersing ourselves in a familiar or enjoyable setting, we may be able to escape the pain.

For many of us, calming our mind begins by recalling a particular place or time in our life which symbolizes safety, comfort, warmth, or pleasure. We can imagine ourselves being in that special place, remembering all the sights and sounds, colors and smells, textures and feelings associated with that setting. The more detailed our fantasy, the more relaxed we may feel. To journey away from today can give us deep rest.

Since we can only hold one image in our mind at a time, an alternate, positive image can replace our pain. We can temporarily escape.

When I'm in need of calmness or retreat I will escape to a safe and special place in my mind.

Going On

"I will go on because I have to; how I go on is up to me. I have much more strength than I believe I have. I must take it a day at a time, and remember that the 'gift' of suffering is to make me better and stronger."

Adina Wrobleski, in loving memory of her daughter, Lynn Oja Wrobelski, who died by suicide.

In the early days and weeks after our loved one's death, we often wonder if we can make it: until the next hour, the next day, the next week. We may have little strength or energy, and even our will to live may be very low at times. The despair and sadness overpowers us. No one can take these intense emotions away, make us better magically, or give us the will to go on. Yet that is what we often seek.

As Adina shares, she came to realize it was up to her to find a way to go on, to put one foot in front of another, to find her strength and use it. No one can do this for us. The will to live, to find reasons to go on, comes from within us and grows when we find support from others. We may find we have more inner strength than we thought, and it may help to remember that we do not have to set goals for months ahead; we can set our sights on much closer goals. Our goal can be to make it to tomorrow, or to find one reason to live for today.

I can go on. I can make it to tomorrow. I will take things one day at a time, seeking and using my inner strength.

Anger With Our Loved One

"I am angry with him for dying. It's such a foolish waste. My children will never know their grandfather."

> Lisa Harvey, in memory of her father, Ed Flannery.

Whether our loved one died suddenly and unexpectedly or after a prolonged illness, we may find ourselves angry at them for leaving us. Their death may seem like such a senseless loss; they had so much more to share, to do. We may tell ourselves that it wasn't their fault or something they could control. Or, maybe we feel they could have exerted some power to have stayed alive. This feeling can be especially strong in cases of suicide, accidents, or deaths due to habits or addictions such as drinking and smoking.

Most of us feel this anger at some time or another; it comes from our deep love for them. When we feel this way, their death seems like such a waste. They had so much yet to give. Rather than bottling this feeling inside of us, we may find some relief by letting it come out.

I can be angry with my loved one and feel cheated by their death. If my heart leads me to believe that they had a part in causing their death, I will allow the anger to be there and then work towards forgiving them. When I am ready, I will let the anger flow through me and bring it outside of my body and heart.

Control

*"I learned a lot about life this week
and how quickly it can be taken away.
The plans that we make for tomorrow
can be easily cancelled today.
We have no control over some things,
although often we think that we might."*

Bonnie Wolf, in memory of her daughter,
Molly Wilma Lynn.

"Control" is a word most of us can relate to. We often feel more secure when we can control things in our lives, and most of us don't like to be out of control at all. We may believe that if we eat healthy foods, exercise, and maintain a positive attitude, then we will have healthy babies, live long lives, and get much of what we want from life.

Yet unexpected losses and unusual circumstances happen; disease, illness, and death occur despite our every effort. These out-of-control events hit us hard. We look for causes both within and outside ourselves, partly because we want to once again feel in control. The truth is that we are not as powerful and influential as we might like, however hard that is to accept. When fate is out of our control, our feelings of being vulnerable mount.

Letting go of our need to control will ease our burden, and accepting where we are without placing blame may help us find inner calm.

I will remind myself that I am not in total control of my life, my family, or this world. I can let go of controlling one aspect of my life today.

Restlessness

"Sleep was a luxury that eluded me night after night."
Linda Taylor Williams, in loving memory of her husband.

Many of us go through periods of extreme restlessness after our loved one dies. We may crave sleep, but no matter how hard we try, it evades us time and time again. We feel frustrated and irritated. We yearn for deep and satisfying rest.

Often, sleep eludes us because our mind is racing and we can't quiet or calm it down. Rather than continually berating ourselves for not sleeping or telling ourselves that we should or have to sleep, we need to let go. We must trust that our body can take care of itself, naturally. Sometimes it helps to write down our thoughts, drink a warm beverage, or listen to soothing music. By letting go, we will find that sleep returns.

I will not pressure myself to get sleep. I will trust my body's natural process.

Feeling Physically Drained
from Emotional Pain

"During those first few days and weeks I remember wondering what was happening to me. I sat around and sighed continuously, experiencing such a tightness in my chest and heaviness in my heart that it was difficult to breathe at times. My nose and face hurt so much from crying I could hardly stand it."

Anonymous

Our bodies may ache, especially our faces and chests; even our hearts seem to hurt from our grief. The strain of our emotions comes out through our body.

These common responses to deep pain can be frightening to us, especially if we have rarely felt something this intensely. Yet they *will* eventually ease and someday become a memory, smoothed over by time and our grieving. But for now, we must find ways to weather this storm and to take care of ourselves as best we can.

On the days when I am physically drained and in pain emotionally, I will accept these symptoms as normal responses to my grief. I can seek momentary release by doing something special, like taking a hot bath or shower, sitting in the sun, reading a good book, or writing.

Intimacy

"I feel vulnerable. I would like the warmth and intimacy of sex, but I'm afraid. I'm not sure if or when I'll be ready."

Anonymous

Thoughts of becoming intimate again can be scary and confusing for many of us. On the one hand, we may crave the tenderness and closeness that lovemaking provides. Yet we may not feel ready to be close with another person and open to such vulnerability.

For many, making love requires a high level of emotional commitment. If we feel emotionally bound to our loved one, we may not feel free to share our affection with another person right now. For the time being, we may need to fill our desire for intimacy and physical contact in other ways. Asking a family member for a hug, holding hands with a friend, or seeking companionship from a pet can help satisfy our need.

It's okay if I'm not ready to make love yet. I can fill my need to be intimate in other ways for the time being.

Bargaining with God

"My grandfather passed away one week after my grandmother. I was eleven years old at the time, and was convinced I had caused their deaths by not being a better person in God's eyes. I wanted to strike up some sort of bargain with Him to stop any more bad from happening."

Mary Bacon Elver, in loving memory of her grandparents.

Our loved one's death has brought agony and suffering to our life. We worry that such adversity will plague us again and again. Many turn to God, pleading with Him to halt the onslaught of pain and sorrow. In reasoning with Him, many of us assume the responsibility for what has happened and offer to be better—better parents, spouses, friends, or children. Or, we promise to try harder—go to church more often, read the Bible more frequently, quit smoking, or get straight "A"s. Through bargaining, we hope to persuade God to stop the bad from happening to us.

Offering to be better or try harder does not guarantee a future without suffering. If our heart leads us to goodness, there need be no strings attached. Living each day fully is what's important.

Instead of trying to bargain for a future without suffering, I will appreciate today for all it brings.

Feelings Breaking Through

"In the days and weeks following our friend Colleen's death, we let all the arrangements and planning consume us and swallow us up. Frankly, we just couldn't bear to get in touch with the terrible sense of shock and grief we felt over her sudden death. Being distracted let us avoid reality a while, but then one day the dam that had been holding in our feelings broke."

Curt and Elizabeth Levang, in memory of their valued friend, Colleen Kent.

There are a great many tasks that must be attended to when a loved one dies, from handling financial matters to putting away their possessions. For some of us, these tasks become all-consuming activities, occupying every minute of our days and leaving little time to dwell on the death of our loved one or feel the intensity of their loss.

Whatever our reasons for being distracted, the dam eventually breaks. For many, the break comes after several days of being especially emotional and crying over minor things. We may have dropped a cup, lost a phone number, or had a disagreement with a friend and sobbed uncontrollably in response. Our crying over these little things signals the rush of emotions that may soon be upon us. Our grief and sorrow were never far away.

It's okay that I have been distracted. I won't be surprised when little disappointments or frustrations lead me to a deeper sorrow and grief for my loved one.

Changing Emotions

"The pain is still very fresh. I'm feeling many of the common reactions: I feel guilty at times, angry at times, and disbelieving at others. At many other times, I'm jealous of people who have babies."

Kimberly D. Lay, in loving memory of her precious daughter, Lucinda.

Many feelings come and go in the early days and weeks of grieving over the loss of our loved one. Anger may be overtaken by guilt, then by total disbelief, jealousy, or envy. This emotional overload is something each of us can relate to; it is a real part of new grief. It seems to happen in spite of every effort to control it, which may make it seem even more frightening.

This flood of emotions can lead to mental and physical strain, creating an even heavier burden. When our feelings are supported and validated by others, we may be able to better accept that they are a part of us, at least for now. Then we won't have to spend so much time fighting them or fearing them—we will know we are not crazy. These changing emotions *are* normal. This realization may make them a bit easier to bear, though it may not lessen their intensity.

When I feel overwhelmed with emotions, I will work towards accepting my feelings, rather than trying to control or fear them. I will remind myself that grief brings these emotions as a response to the pain and the love I am feeling.

Drug and Alcohol Use

"At first, I dealt with death by repressing my feelings and trying to forget my loss. This was a mistake and caused me a multitude of problems, one of which was a serious addiction to alcohol and drugs. I have since learned how to deal with my loss. I don't have to like it, but I can learn to accept it and not let it affect every other aspect of my life."

Ken Pugh, in memory of his loved ones.

We all cope with the loss of a loved one differently. Some of us confront the pain and anguish directly, drawing support and comfort from our friends and family. Others, like Ken, may first try to run from their feelings by anesthetizing themselves with drugs or alcohol. However, escaping into a blurred world of nothingness only stops or hides some of our pain. The false respite doesn't last forever, and it can't end all our suffering. Eventually, we have to *feel our pain.* Sadly, attempts at numbing ourselves only prolong our grief.

Drinking or taking drugs only offers me temporary relief. I will attempt to do the grieving I need to do, seeking other means of support.

Absent Mindedness

"I was forgetful and disinterested in routine chores during the weeks following the death of my husband. I used to be so organized and have a sharp mind. Yet I found myself forgetting what people told me, I couldn't pay my bills, getting meals was impossible, and I forgot where I put things. In fact, anything that came up seemed to overwhelm me. It was very humbling to rely on people to help me—my mind was so consumed by the grief."

> *Michele Borden, in loving memory of her husband, Ted.*

Disinterest in the routine tasks of daily living is something most of us experience at some time or another following a crisis. This seems especially true during the early weeks of our loved one's death. Our mind naturally has a hard time concentrating in the middle of our trauma and turmoil. Paying bills, opening mail, or making meals can seem unimportant and difficult to do. Yet by not handling these responsibilities, we can actually make our lives more complicated and troubled.

When possible, we need to allow others to help us. In fact, we may need to be very specific by asking for assistance with particular problems, like legal matters or the maintenance of our home. And if we have neglected some important aspect of daily life, such as paying bills, it may be helpful to talk with the affected party. Most often, they will be understanding if we explain that we have suffered a death in the family.

If I am overwhelmed with the daily tasks of living, I will remember that others have faced this same problem. I can ask for help from relatives, friends, and any affected party.

Feeling the Pain

"We have allowed ourselves to feel the pain of our very empty arms and have found that to be the secret to healing our broken heart."

> *Debbie Crippen, in loving memory of her son, Justin, who lived two days.*

Facing the long, lonely tunnel of grief after the death of a loved one is quite frightening. We may wonder if we can make it. We may wish to take a short cut, or try to find ways to avoid the tough trek. This is understandable. The journey is intense, it is lonely, and it is hard work.

When we are able, we might try to face the pain, to let it flow through our bodies and our hearts. It may be expressed through our tears or words, by writing, drawing, playing music, or through more active physical activities; whatever way seems right for us. When we face the pain, it may feel like we are allowing the river of mourning to sweep us away, trying in vain to keep from being washed down an overpowering stream. Though there will be days when we cannot confront this feeling, maybe today is the day we can go with the stream's natural flow, allowing the pain and feelings of grief to wash over us. We can trust that this may be one of the secrets to healing.

I can float with the stream today. I can feel what is inside me. I can seek ways to express what is within.

Coping In Our Own Way

"Overwhelmed, confused, short of breath. I feel as though I am drowning in sorrow. For now, I want to just sit with her pictures and remember for hours at a time. But friends think I should try to be happy and put the mementos away."

> *Rebecca Keating, in loving memory of her mother, Ruthe Grace Keating.*

When we are coping in our own way, others need to respect that, even if they think there is a better way. When someone is drowning and struggling in the water, it's not the time to teach them a new stroke.

Friends, relatives, and co-workers want to help us. Sometimes, however, they don't know how. In an attempt to offer support, they may offer all sorts of advice. They might tell us to "ask for help whenever you need it," "put it behind you," "keep busy and don't think about it," or "go ahead and cry."

At this difficult time we may feel like we are treading water, using the strokes that work best for now. We need to trust our judgment about the needs and options we believe will help, then seek moral support to help us follow through.

If we are feeling stuck, confused, or troubled, we may want to consider the coping tips others suggest. However, we may be better prepared to learn new coping techniques when we are more steady on our feet. If we feel we need help, it is important to call a clergy person, physician, or counselor for some assistance.

Though I realize that there may be other ways to handle this crisis, right now I am doing the best I can. I will keep using my good judgment about what is working for me, yet try to remain open to the advice of others.

Disappointment When Others Seem Insensitive

"I think the very worst thing for me was that no one really seemed to care. Only one couple from my church even sent me a card. I felt abandoned and like a freak of sorts. Hardly anyone called. I felt hurt and bewildered."
Vicki Campbell, in memory of her child.

It can be disappointing when others don't support us as we had hoped following our loved one's death. We may have expected our clergy, co-workers, friends, and relatives to be there for us. If people avoided us, didn't speak directly about the loss and our feelings, or if they stopped coming by shortly after our loss, we may feel abandoned and hurt. This avoidance and apparent insensitivity adds to our pain and heartache.

We may wonder whether others don't care about us or about our loved one's death. In reality, there may be many reasons why they seem distant and unsupportive. Many people don't know how to openly support us, and they may not understand our needs at this moment. They may be afraid of hurting us more, so they use silence and avoidance as their way of offering support. Though they may not realize it, their silence may be a way of protecting themselves from our pain, and from their own.

I can feel disappointed when others seem to have abandoned me or appear insensitive to my loss. I will try to understand that they are struggling to help, but don't know how. I can tell them what I need.

Questions of Faith

"I had believed God to be a loving father. Maybe someday I can believe in Him again. If and when I do, I know it will be because I have built a different scaffolding of beliefs. I will have gone through each of my beliefs, sifting through them carefully, before I entrust any strength to them."

> *Mary Van Bockern, in loving memory of her daughter, Catherine Mary, who died at age three.*

Whether God has been a stable force in our lives or an infrequent guest, many of us rely on Him for guidance and protection. But when our loved one is suddenly gone from us, we may challenge our former view of God and our faith. We may feel angry, cheated, confused, bitter, helpless, and even hopeless. From the onerous weight of our loss we may cry out, "Where are you, God? Why have you brought such horrible pain into my life?"

Suffering can test our faith. It may prompt us to seriously ask ourselves what and in whom we believe. We may question the lessons we learned as young children, or struggle with the doctrine and beliefs embraced by our families and churches. For many, this may be the first time we have allowed ourselves to doubt or question God. This struggle is natural and under-standable. It may take us time to sort out how the loss of our loved one has affected our beliefs.

I can question God and my faith. I do not have to hide my confusion, anger, disappointment, or other feelings. I will give myself time to think, and not rush towards immediate answers.

Remembering Our Loved One's
Virtues and Faults

"Gram was so special, always giving and sharing herself with others. She was the best Grandmother a person could have. Most of the time I can't think of anything I would have changed. Then there are days when I recall her imperfections, and I feel guilty for even thinking of them."

Sherokee Ilse, in memory of her grandmother, Genevieve Kriesch.

When someone we love dies it is common to revere them, magnifying their good points. We remember the happy times and their special gifts. It almost seems disloyal to even think of the bad times or any of their faults. We miss them and have a desire to focus on the good in them.

While this is certainly acceptable and normal, it is also understandable that occasionally, conflicting memories of their less than perfect qualities will surface. We may feel guilty for thinking these things, but they can't be stopped. No one is perfect, and both the good times and the bad times become the treasures they have left us.

When I think of my loved one I will remember their special qualities. If troubling memories surface, I will face them and allow them to remain. I need not feel guilty for either glorifying or being critical of my loved one.

Controlling Chaos

"After my husband's death, everything turned upside down. I had to make some sense out of the chaos. Everything had to be in order. I was obsessed by order. I spent hours, days, and weeks getting the finances in order, organizing cupboards, closests and anything else I could find."

Maggie Merkow, in loving memory of her husband, Rob.

Chaos, confusion, and a sense of disorder may follow our loved one's death. Our once sensible world may feel like it has turned upside down. Where we once may have had order, routine and control, we now may feel like we have little or no control, especially when it comes to our emotions.

Maggie admits that she was obsessed with bringing order to her chaos. Although this was not her normal personality style, it became a coping and survival technique for her.

Each of us seek ways to deal with the feeling of chaos. We may find ourselves behaving differently than we normally do. This may be confusing to others, but if it feels right or seems necessary at the time, we need to trust our judgment and instincts.

When I feel that my life has become chaotic, I will do what I need to do in order to feel some sense of control.

Expressing Grief

*"Grief needs to sob aloud; grief does not want to smile;
grief has to serve its inner healing first."*

> *sascha, in loving memory of Eve and Nino
> Hendee, her splendid children.*

The grief that automatically overcomes us when our
loved one dies needs to be expressed. In order to move
beyond it, we need to move through it. The tears, sobs,
and sadness that surround and overtake us are healing
in their own way. Rather than trying to be strong, to hide
our responses, maybe we can allow ourselves to wallow
in sadness and even self-pity for awhile. We need not
put on a false face for ourselves or others. After all, we
loved this person very much, it only makes sense that we
will grieve their loss deeply. We will be true to ourselves
and the healing process of grief by facing the pain and
expressing it.

*I will allow the feelings of grief to come from
within me. This inner healing will not be
painless. By expressing it, I will be sharing my
love and pain with the hope that the future will
be better.*

Is God Punishing Me?

"I went over and over the details of the last several weeks and months. What had I done to deserve this? I thought I had been living the best life I could. I felt God was punishing me, but for what?"

> Pamela J. Arens, in loving memory of her dad, Edsel Ford Bonser.

When the life of a loved one ends, we may wonder what we did to deserve such tragedy. We may worry that we are being punished for some unnamed sin or terrible misdeed. We may question if our loss is a test of our strength, our faith, or our love of God. Is there a purpose to our suffering? A lesson God wants us to learn?

The thought of being punished by God may haunt us at one time or another as we grieve. Separating ourselves from what has happened is difficult, and so it is understandable that we look inward to justify this painful event. Yet we all know of instances where good people have lost loved ones tragically, and we do not think that God is punishing them. We should not judge ourselves more harshly than we judge others.

It is not helpful to think that I am being punished for the way I have lived my life. I can let go of these thoughts. Today, I will recall a few unselfish acts of kindness that I have extended to others.

Filling the Void

"I don't think we should try to forget...the particular hole left by a loved one will never be filled and we shouldn't try to fill it. To grieve is to feel...love...live. Grieving is a part of living."

Jill Cerulli, in loving memory of her mom and dad.

One of the most troubling aspects of a loss is the tremendous void that is suddenly created. Believing and accepting that the person we loved is gone is painful and difficult. Some of us try to find ways to fill the void so that we can hide from our grief, or at least keep it at bay. Yet with time we find that the void isn't something we can fill and running from our grief doesn't work. Sad as it may be, we need to grieve. Grieving is a normal human response and we must let it take its course, wherever that may be.

Even though there is a void, I will not attempt to fill it. I will let myself grieve.

64   *The Early Weeks*

Feeling Helpless to Support Others

"When my husband finally broke down and cried in my arms I felt so loved and needed. Yet also so helpless."
     Cathy Sullivan, in memory of her son, Darrel Dominic.

We may find ourselves trying to take care of others after our loved one dies; our partner, parent, child, relative, or friend. We want to keep their pain to a minimum, and caring for them helps us stay busy so we don't have to face our own pain. Yet when others seek our support or show their vulnerabilty, we can feel so helpless. We can't take their pain away any more than we can our own. It may feel like we have failed them.

We may need to reevaluate our role in trying to support someone. Just *being* with someone in pain is very important. Our presence and compassion can bring consolation and support.

When I attempt to help others who are also hurting, I will remember that I cannot take their pain away, only be with them. This *is* being helpful to them.

Being Avoided by Others

"Everyone avoided me. Nobody knew what to say. I felt like I had the plague and was contagious. (I still feel that way.) I imagined that when I left the house, eyes were peering at me through shuttered windows."

Hanell Nelson, in loving memory of her daughter, Amy.

Sometimes it may seem as if people think we have a rare, highly contagious disease and they shouldn't get too close to us. They may avoid us in shopping centers, on the street, or in church or at the synagogue. This isolation adds to our loneliness and the concern we may already have that something is wrong with us.

What we may crave in such a distressful time is closeness, the love and warm embrace of people who care about us. Distance and avoidance can hurt. To counteract this pain, we need to express our feelings and find ways to let our disappointment and frustrations out.

When I feel lonely and isolated I will seek understanding friends who are willing to be there for me. Sadness shared is sadness lessened.

Living in the Present

"One of the important things to remember when grieving is to try to live in the present."

*from **A Gift of Hope: How We Survive Our Tragedies**, by Robert Veninga.*

After our loved one's death, we often worry about the future or have regrets about the past. Such feelings are understandable and may at times even be helpful. However, if healing is to occur, we must also give our attention to the present. As Robert suggests, instead of dwelling on the past or lamenting the lost future, it is beneficial to also focus on today and affirm those strengths that are deep within us.

Today I will focus on the present. I have many strengths inside me which I will affirm and use in coping with my loved one's death.

Exhaustion Comes and Goes

"Exhaustion.
It now engulfs me
in a sea of endless sadness and tears."
    from **The Anguish of Loss** *by Julie Fritsch, in loving memory of her son, Justin.*

Mourning the loss of a loved one is exhausting and consuming. A great amount of energy goes into coping and just 'making it' from one minute to the next, especially during the early weeks. Many of us have trouble getting out of bed, answering the phone, or doing daily tasks. Feeling tired and worn out is a natural reaction to what can seem to be an almost unbearable nightmare.

Even after some time has passed, coping with daily life can still be exhausting. As waves of grief come and go, they can overwhelm our emotional and physical selves. There are still likely to be days when getting out of bed is difficult, and when little things touch off our sorrow. Thankfully, this doesn't last forever.

When I am feeling exhausted I will remind myself that this is a natural response to the hard work of grieving, loving, and letting go. I will rest and take care of myself on these days.

Accepting Reality

"There were so many moments in those first few weeks of my uncle's death that I just naturally thought about phoning to check and see how he was feeling. But, before I even had the telephone in my hand, I would remember that he was dead."

Elizabeth Levang, in loving memory of her uncle, Tony Rizzo.

There are times when we momentarily forget that our loved one has died. Then, reality steps in and forces us to remember what is true. Though reality may appear to be harsh and unfeeling, it is the compass which keeps us on track. We can learn to rely on this vital directional guide as it aids us on our journey to a greater sense of peace and normalcy.

There may be times when I forget that my loved one has died. I will look to reality to help me accept what is true.

Being Thankful for Our Loved One's Life

"After my daughter died, I received a card that will always stick in my mind. My friend Ann wrote, 'the pain of losing her must be great, but maybe the pain of never experiencing her might have been worse.' How true that is! I wouldn't have given up my short time with her for anything. We will all love and remember her forever."

Michele Prekker, in loving memory of her daughter, Mallory.

In many ways, we all would have liked to wish our tragedy away, to never have felt the heartache of our loss. Yet which would we prefer: that they never lived, and therefore could not have died, or the path we are on now?

Most of us come to a place in our grief, sometimes very early, when we can feel thankful for the time we shared with our loved one. Their contributions to our life have been immeasurable, and although it can sometimes be hard to keep this in mind as we grieve, the experience of knowing and loving them is worth all the pain we must suffer.

I can find thankfulness for my loved one's life. I can find moments when their specialness overshadows my pain and heartache.

Searching for a Loved One

"Longing comes again in this darkness
I quietly slip from my bed
and follow
What am I following?
The beating of my own heart?
I am searching, looking for what is lost.
Where do I find you, my son?
This longing consumes me and I weep

The morning sun finds me
    tearstained and exhausted
And gently urges me to begin another day"
        Patti Fochi, in loving memory of her son, Justin.

The longing and searching for our loved one touches us deeply, until we are abruptly reminded that they are gone. We have lost much since their death: their touch, their smell, the essence of this human being we loved dearly. We want to believe they are only gone for the moment, to return tonight, or tomorrow. The searching and hoping continues, in spite of the harshness of reality that sometimes strikes us in the face.

Yet we need not look too far for them. They are forever within our hearts.

As I search for my loved one, I will hold the harsh realities at bay. I miss them and love them. When I am ready, I can look within my own heart and life, for they are with me always.

The Slowness of Time

"At first everyone told me it takes time, but I couldn't wait! I wished the weeks and months away, but time was too slow."

> Susan and Fred Stewart, in loving memory of their son, Travis Fred.

Time may seem like our greatest enemy. Relatives and friends may tell us, "it takes time to heal," "time will make things better," or "just give it time." Yet in the beginning, each minute seems like forever. We want time to go by more quickly, wishing we could move the calendar ahead a year or more in hopes that we will be all better by then.

It's hard to be patient and let time pass. It's also a mistake to think that time alone will make us better. The day to day effort of grieving and remembering over a period of time is how we heal. In the newness of grief, days may seem endless. But after awhile, instead of measuring our progress and time in minutes, hours, and days, we will find ourselves talking of weeks, and eventually months. In the meantime, the journey is painful, and time seems to pass very slowly.

I can be impatient with time today.

Feeling Their Presence

"As I embrace the gift of my living daughter and surround myself with her laughter and beauty, I still feel the presence of my older child, my son. He is a part of our family, even if only in spirit, and to me his existence can never be denied."

> Mayrse Wilde, in memory of her son, Ricky-Adrian.

As we grieve, many of us can feel the spirit and presence of our loved one who has died. They remain an important member of our family. Someone's laugh, smile, or manner of speaking may remind us of them. Traditional family gatherings, celebrations, or even joyful moments in a day bring them to mind. In the very happiness of loving others, intimate and warm feelings for our loved one keeps them close.

I can appreciate the specialness of my living family. At times this specialness brings me closer to my loved one who has died. I will remember their spirit and seek their presence in my life.

Stress

"Ever since my Dad's death, I've felt so much pressure. The stress feels like it keeps building and never goes away."

Anonymous

Our lives were already complicated, so when our loved one dies, the normal stresses may seem to multiply. We may feel tense and anxious, our feelings of distress coming from being pulled in so many directions. Burdened by the many responsibilities, we can feel frazzled and worn out.

Often, stress is a reaction to a strained and unhealthy lifestyle. Our bodies may be telling us to slow down and take better care of ourselves. For now, we may need to relinquish some of our responsibilities and make time for ourselves. Though this may seem selfish, it must be done. For if we fail to take care of ourselves, we may find our lives getting even more out of control.

When I feel stressed I will reassess my commitments and diligently set priorities in order to take care of myself. I can do something nice for myself today.

The Uneven Path

Living When A Loved One Has Died
by Rabbi Dr. Earl A. Grollman

Don't try to destroy a beautiful
part of your life because
remembering hurts.
As children of today and tomorrow,
we are also children of yesterday.
The past still travels with us
and what it has been
makes us what we are.

Putting Off Until Tomorrow

"The enormity of burying my child has gradually begun to sink in; I may never fully grasp it. Nor do I want to. I just don't have the energy to think about it right now—this is my reaction to so many things. I'll think about it tomorrow."

Jan Pease, in loving memory of her son, Nathaniel Edward.

Most of the decisions and feelings that follow a death demand a level of energy and intensity that can be overwhelming. Whether the task is taking care of our loved one's belongings or making decisions about our job, home, or our children, at times we may feel incapable of even trying. We may be wise to let these thoughts go today and think about them tomorrow. This will allow reality to sink in slowly, and keep us somewhat insulated for awhile longer.

If I am overwhelmed or unable to think about something right now I will set it aside for tomorrow or another day.

Special Memories and Mementos

"My life has been filled with a storehouse of experiences that my Mom made possible—those wonderful visits to Chicago to be with her family, all the celebrations she put together... When I look back, I say 'Thanks for the memories, Mom.'"

Julie Faxvog, in memory of her mother, Charlotte Margaret Joan Doherty Klug, who died three days after Christmas.

At Charlotte Klug's funeral service, her granddaughters brought a number of mementos to the altar: a worn deck of playing cards, a framed family picture, an oversized Raggedy Ann doll, a handknit Christmas stocking, and a small glass jar of cherries. While these may seem like rather ordinary items, each memento represented an important piece of Charlotte's life. Charlotte delighted in making banana splits, and for her, a banana split was never complete without a bright red cherry sitting on top. To Charlotte's family, Grandma was the best of all card players, always willing to deal just one more hand.

Special possessions may forever bring with them thoughts of our loved one. These mementos may become the tender remnants of a life history. They can trigger sights, sounds, smells, and sensations which are imbedded in our mind. We can hold dear to these special items.

I will take a moment to think about a few of my special possessions and the memories tied to them.

Pretending Everything is Okay

"My friends often ask me how I am doing. I want to tell them to please stop asking for awhile. Some days I need to go on as if this has not happened. I pretend I'm okay so that I can deal with the issues of living."

LaVerne Ziegenfuss, in loving memory of Barbara Williams.

There may be days when we need to not think about what is missing, but rather focus on what is happening today in our lives. This may be good to do, especially if we have been focusing on our pain and sorrow for a very long time. It's okay to act like it's behind us, whether for a few days or a little longer. This can be a helpful coping tool. What is probably most important is that we search within ourselves to determine what we need today to cope.

I can trust my feelings and instincts. I know what I need to do in order to cope and survive. If it feels helpful, I can focus on living for today.

Unsettled Conflicts and Strain
Over Funeral Arrangements

"My brother and I wanted to say or do something special at my sister's funeral, a prayer or testimonial. My parents asked us not to. They wanted the family together during the service. At the time, it seemed appropriate to follow their will. I didn't question it then and I don't regret it now. However, there are times I can't help but wonder if our grieving process would have been different if we had been allowed to share in this service."

Pastor Mike Zylstra, in loving memory of his sister Mary, who died in a car accident.

Our loved one's funeral or memorial service might have been a stressful time. Family members might all have different ideas about how the service was to be planned, and disagreements or quarrels might have ensued. Emotionally, this was a taxing time for us, and to keep peace, we might have decided to let the wishes of others override our own desires.

Trying to minimize the strain and keep the family together is an honorable goal. Yet if we have any regrets or harbor any resentments about the funeral, it's best not to let them fester too long. We can tell our family what we wanted and why, and how we are feeling about it now. By expressing our feelings in a positive way we can move toward forgiveness.

If I am still feeling unsettled or disappointed about my loved one's funeral or memorial service, I will tell my family. I can choose not to harbor resentments.

Surviving the "Whys"

"Blinded by my own tears, I could hardly see the medical examiners bring down the body of my dearest friend from her apartment building on the day she had been murdered. Why her? Why! The questions kept piercing my heart and I thought I too would die along with her. She had been a woman of strong faith and conviction. Her love covered our neighborhood. Her friendship and fellowship had brought me through many struggles in the years I had come to know and love her. Her murder had been a senseless one."

    Catrina Ganey, in loving memory of Michelle Rougeau.

Anger, loss, and confusion crowd around us when someone we love dies a tragic and sudden death. There are no books to read or courses to take to adequately prepare for such a tragedy. There are no answers to the question that keeps plaguing us: "Why?" It's hard to believe that just the other day, hour, or moment we were talking, laughing, or playing together, making plans for our future. Now they are gone.

Sometimes it is important for us not to look at how we are going to survive the day, but rather at what we will do to survive the moment. Our entire system has suffered a shock. Giving ourselves permission to grieve in our own way and at our own pace can help lessen the blow over time.

I can do something special today to survive the moments: write in my journal, go for a walk, notice the clouds in the sky, say a prayer, or think of one thing I am thankful for.

The Uneven Path

Intense and Overwhelming Feelings

"After my mother's death, I was a confused, passive, dependent, suicidal individual; and I was scared!"
Laure Janus, in loving memory of her mother.

Many of the feelings we experience in our grief are new to us. We may never have felt quite this confused or anxious before, and it scares us. We fear we will always feel this way, and life will never be better. Feeling hopeless, we may consider death as the only way to elude our pain, and thoughts of suicide may enter our mind.

Our grief can overwhelm us to such a degree that we can't seem to look beyond today. This narrow focus exaggerates the negatives, and we may be unable to see that tomorrow could be different. For now, we need to put life in perspective. This is not the time to make impulsive decisions. Our life has had meaning in the past, and there is no reason to believe that it won't in the future. Thoughts of suicide are a sign of desperation. If we reach this point, it is important to tell someone we trust and to seek professional help.

I can honestly admit how great my pain is and how scared I feel. I do have things to live for. I can look for value and meaning in my life. If I feel desperate, I will seek help immediately.

God's Concern for Others

"It was bad enough that I lost a husband, but I hurt so much for my four children; they no longer had a dad. It broke my heart. But when I looked to the Lord, He said "It breaks my heart, too." My overriding feeling is one of thankfulness to Him. I feel like my four children and I are a miracle of God's grace."

Michele Borden, in loving memory of her husband, Ted.

We may have strong concerns for those who are also affected by our tragedy: the children, siblings, parents, or surviving partner of our loved one who has died. Our heart aches for them. We may question God's wisdom and plan—why he would allow such a thing to happen? Why do so many have to hurt so much?

Michele was able to understand that the Lord's heart was broken, too. She wasn't alone, nor was she or her loved ones being punished by an unloving God. Through all of her agony her faith stood fast, even through all the anguish and despair. Over time she felt God's grace and His pain, and her relationship with Him became even stronger.

I can believe in God's grace. I can trust that His heart also broke with my loved one's death, and that He cares for all who are now in sorrow.

Working in a Daze

"There were entire days at work where I merely functioned in a daze. I could not remember from hour to hour what I had done or what I would do next. I simply dealt with each situation as it arose and muddled through it. I'm relatively sure that on the surface I appeared okay to my co-workers and customers, but on the inside I was coming apart."

> Tim Nelson, in loving memory of his daughter, Kathleen.

Attempting to work and function normally while still feeling the effects of our loved one's death can be the ultimate challenge. We need to go on, keep working, and put on a professional face for our employer and the public. Yet we may feel we are falling apart on the inside, working in a daze. This double role can wear us down.

We may need to make sure we have support in the other aspects of our life; socially, emotionally, physically, and spiritually, to provide balance and energy.

If I find myself working in a daze, putting up a front at work to get the job done, I will allow myself to do that. At the same time, I will take good care of myself.

Unfairness of Life

"In our despair, life seems so unfair.
A period is placed in the middle of the sentence,
*   Instead of at the end.*
All earthly dreams and plans we're forced to suspend.
We say, 'This can't be so—we can't let this child go.'
It's impossible to understand
*   What is completely out of our hands."*
        Betty Stallings, in loving memory of her dear
son, David Ryan.

Many of us grew up expecting that life would be fair. We believed that working hard and leading a proper life would banish all anguish, sorrow, and suffering from our door. But when our loved one dies, we suddenly find that life's harshness has not left us unscathed.

Life can feel cruel and terribly unfair. The inconsistencies can be hard to understand. Our once wonderful vision of life may now stand in silent contrast to what life has actually brought. We may never have been promised that life would be fair, but most of us had hoped and dreamt it would be.

My vision of life is not what I had imagined. I will slowly try to let go of it, and accept this new reality.

Guilt Over Feeling Happy

"I smiled today. I laughed out loud. I shouldn't feel happy. Should I?"

Jill Bresnahan, in loving memory of her mother, Elaine Swanson.

We may feel guilty and confused about how we *ought* to be responding to our loved one's death. The extreme emotions of grief take a good deal of energy, and may leave us feeling depressed and withdrawn. Our body, spirit, and mind may need a break from the work of grieving, so humor and happiness, even if momentary, are vital to our health.

I will look for a bit of humor or happiness today, even if only for the moment. I need to be renewed.

Will I Survive?

"Why... Why! Pain—how can one have this much pain and still be alive?"

Joyce Barga, in loving memory of her son, Christopher Lee, who was killed in a car accident.

As we stagger under the great weight of our pain we may wonder if we will be able to survive. How much can we bear, and for how long? Is there no limit to what the human spirit can stand?

Regretably, there are no boundaries to our pain. No one can say for certain how heavy our load will be or when the pain will stop. For now, we must take small steps, one day at a time. Finding others to share our burdens and our pain may help lighten our load.

The weight of my pain sometimes feels oppressive. No one can tell me how long all this will last, but for now I will live one day at a time.

Coping With the Family's Grief

"It was rough telling the other children that their older brother was dead. They so loved and adored him. Being so young, they didn't really understand what death was all about. One son refused to talk about it at all, while another has done well, drawing pictures of him with little wings on them. It's been hard to deal with my grief and theirs too."

Anonymous

Helping other family members, especially children, understand and cope with death is very difficult. Feeling shaken and vulnerable ourselves makes the task doubly hard.

Since grief is such an individual process, we must be careful about our expectations. Encouraging family members to be open and honest about their feelings and willing to support each other is important right now. Setting an example by our own behavior may be a valuable first step.

Our loved one's death is a trying time for our entire family; we must try to be patient, understanding, and respectful of everyone's need to grieve in their own way. Finding ways for the family to pull together instead of apart will help to bring healing.

Having to care for my family members in their grief can be difficult. I will let them grieve in their own way and not place high expectations on them. Today I will think of one thing to do that will help keep my family together rather than split it apart.

A Broken Heart

"Our son Wayne was hit by a train near our home. Our son was dead from an accident at the age of seventeen! I thought I would die right along with him, from a broken heart."

> Tina McKim, in loving memory of her son, Wayne.

Initially, the death of a loved one tends to obscure good memories and takes away inner peace. The fear of living without them may be so great that we may feel we will be unable to survive. Our broken heart affects every fiber of our body. We may find it hard to sleep, or we may embrace it as a means to escape the pain. We may have no appetite, or we may eat more than usual, simply to fill the time and keep ourselves distracted. Life can seem so unfair and empty without our loved one.

Yet in time, with the comfort of memories to keep us going, these feelings will diminish. Good support, nonjudgmental listeners, faith, and our deep feelings for our loved one may also help us move through this intense pain.

If my broken heart overwhelms me I will remember that the grief that takes my sleep away at midnight brings me hurt, but it also brings me love. I will open my heart, seeking peace and good memories.

Finding Good Listeners

"I realize it was not only at the beginning, but now, months later, that I need listeners who allow me to talk about what I am experiencing, who listen but do not judge, who do not say what I ought to do."

Carmen Brining, in memory of her son, Tom.

We may be at the point in our grief where we need a good listener or two, a shoulder to lean on. Someone who understands us and our pain. We need those who will confirm and validate our feelings without trying to change them. We have been given plenty of friendly advice and suggestions. But now we may need the comfort that comes from knowing we are not alone, that others can and will mourn with us.

I will seek out a good listener to help me as I mourn. I can turn to a support group, trusted friend, or family member for the shoulder I need.

The Foundation of Our Beliefs

"When I feel sad over my son's death, I picture him in heaven, in the arms of the Lord. I see that my son is not alone. He is cared for in an atmosphere of happiness, surrounded by love. This is a very comforting thought for me."

      Rhonda Grundmeier, in loving memory of her son, Matthew.

Our faith and beliefs can be the framework on which we build our strength. For many of us, our faith provides the courage and reassurance we need to face our loved one's death.

Rhonda knows that the pain she feels is for herself and her family, for all that they are missing. Still, she finds comfort in her heartfelt belief that her son is in heaven.

We can each search within ourselves, examining our own beliefs and faith. The foundation of our beliefs can play a significant part in our grieving and healing process.

If my faith is my strength, through it I can seek the peace and understanding that will help me cope. If the foundation of my beliefs seems shaky, or if I am confused, I can talk with others and share my feelings.

The Warmth of Mother Earth

"When I thought of my child buried in the cold, hard ground I felt tormented and frightened. Then someone spoke to me about the Native American belief that Mother Earth is the warm womb of the world. Now I see Her cradling my child, and my feelings have totally changed. I feel comforted and peaceful."

Anonymous

Native Americans believe that the Great Spirit created the sacred Earthmother to be revered and respected. All of nature is based on the circle: the four seasons, the four directions, and the earth itself. Life, which began from the earth and returns upon death, finds harmony and completion in an unbroken circle. The earth that we walk on is the ashes of our grandfathers, and to desecrate our earth is to desecrate our ancestors. Land and the earth are to be loved, and burial grounds are hallowed and sacred.

Unity with the earth and kinship with all of nature's creatures can bring the vision of warmth and oneness. With this realization, death and burial become a natural part of the continuum, something comforting and peaceful.

I can allow the earth to be a comforting and warm vision as I think of my loved one's body having returned to Mother Earth.

Life on Hold

"Joe and I had been married for quite some time when he died. Now I feel like I'm alone, with little left to look forward to. Quite honestly, I'd rather just die too. My whole life is on hold."

"Mrs. Joe," in memory of her husband and long-time companion.

The feeling of being on hold and wanting to die is a cry of discouragement. Most of us liked our old lives; they may not have been perfect, but they were comfortable and familiar. The prospect of having to create a new life is discouraging. All our dreams and plans for the future may have evaporated with the death of our loved one, and somehow we must begin anew. Sadly, we have little idea how to do this, so dying may sometimes seem like an answer. More than anything, we want our old life back. But we know this is impossible.

Today I will think of one aspect of my life that is not on hold, that positively points to the future. I will embrace this aspect of my life and let it help guide me to the future.

Children's Perceptions

"On a dreary night three weeks after my father died, my dishwasher broke. I collapsed in a heap with my head on the table, sobbing. My husband tried to console me with his plan for fixing the dishwasher. My four-year-old son put his hand on my shoulder and said, 'She's not crying about the dishwasher, she's crying about Grandpa Joe.'"

Donna Damico Mayer, in loving memory of her father, Joseph Damico.

Children can amaze us if we really listen to them and include them in what is happening during these difficult times. The perceptions of Donna's four-year-old may not be unique; it seems that many young children will boldly speak their minds if they feel safe. Yet many people would choose to exclude them from funerals or discussions about a loved one's death.

One of the greatest gifts we can give our children is to respect and love them, especially during this time. Our honesty and openness about what has happened can open doors for them. The gifts they give to us in return—their perceptions, questions, creativity, and honest comments—will make us smile, cry, and perhaps even feel a sense of awe.

The children in my life deserve my openness. I will encourage them to share their feelings and questions in whatever way they are comfortable, whether through words, drawing, music, puppets, or play.

The Comfort of Pets

"When Eric died we discovered just how deep the emotional attachment had been between our boy and his dog. Tammy's behavior left no question in our minds that she was grieving with us. Yet unwittingly, Tammy forced us to face reality, stretched us physically, provided some comic relief when we sorely needed it, and most of all, she loved us with a love that knew no bounds."

Judy Osgood, in loving memory of her son, Eric.

Pets can be a wonderful source of comfort and affection for us. Their love is unconditional and constant. As our trusted and loyal companions, they instinctively share our pain.

How good it feels to have our cat purring on our lap or our dog bound into our arms. Their affection can warm our heart and remind us how much we are loved. In return, these friends give us someone to love and nurture as well. The need to feed and care for them can help us get exercise or break the monotony of an otherwise dreary day. And their antics may give us a chuckle or a smile on those days we need them most.

A pet offers me the chance to both receive and give love. I can welcome the comfort and affection a pet might give.

Depression

"All this pain has changed my values. Before, I always thought of my home and how I could improve something. Things like that are meaningless now. All I can think of is battling the depression and tears and just getting through the day."

Hanell Nelson, in loving memory of her daughter, Amy.

Sometimes our grief becomes overwhelming and turns to depression. Feeling worthless, hopeless, or extremely sad are all signs of this happening. We also may have little or no energy, and even the most routine tasks may seem almost impossible to complete. We would rather just stay in bed, or at home.

In order to move out of our depression, we may need to reassess our attitudes and change our negative thoughts. Instead of withdrawing, we may need to reach out more often. Relying on the sympathetic ear of a friend, getting some exercise, or finding something enjoyable to do, like taking in a movie, may be a first step.

If our depression persists or worsens, we may need to consider getting professional help. Depression is not a sign of weakness. There are times when seeking help is the most courageous and responsible thing we can do for ourselves and our loved ones.

It is important for me to recognize how I'm functioning emotionally. If I feel depressed I will take stock of my attitude and take steps to think differently about life. I can reach out for help if I need it.

Life as a Nightmare

"I feel as if I have been living in a dream, a nightmare to be exact. The days pass and I go through the motions, but I keep pinching myself, waiting to awaken. This is the worst dream I've ever had. Isn't it over yet?"

Elizabeth Morgan, Barbara Curyea, and Kathy Speer, in lasting love for their mother.

We may still find ourselves feeling like we are living a dream. Life may have taken on nightmarish qualities that keep us captive, unable to return to the happier times when we were whole. We may want to go sleep for a long time, hoping that when we wake up, it will be all over. As the days and weeks drag on, the nightmare may continue, reoccurring from time to time. It may help us to know that others have felt this way before, and that these feelings won't last forever. We can survive and find ourselves again.

While I walk in the fog of a dream at times, I will remember that I am not alone, and that in time these feelings will recede.

Facing Our Grief

"To weep is to make less the depth of grief."
*from **King Henry VI**, by William Shakespeare.*

Many of us are afraid to face the pain of our loved one's death. We worry that if we start crying, we'll never stop. Our fear has us teetering on the edge of tears. We are uncomfortable and vulnerable.

We need to let our feelings out. It is only by exposing ourselves to the full intensity of our grief that we will find healing. In the long run, hiding from our grief serves no real purpose.

I will not hide from my grief. I will face it, and as I weep, my grief will lessen.

Saving Our Loved One's Possessions

*"Though it may seem a bit crazy, it becomes difficult to throw away anything our loved one touched. I still have our son's holiday place mat. It's tucked way down below all the other tablecloths in the drawer. I can't—**no, I don't want to**—toss it away. It's ours. It's our grief, our pain, our healing."*

Darcie Sims, in loving memory of her son, Austin.

It's not unusual to retain all sorts of seemingly unimportant objects from our loved one's life along with special possessions. We may save their toothbrush, glasses, crayons, coin purse, or other things that deeply remind us of them. Parting with these things may seem almost disloyal, and nearly unimaginable. They are the reality that confirms that our loved one existed, that they really were alive.

I can save anything or everything that reminds me of my loved one. These objects validate that my loved one was alive.

Anger Growing Into Rage

"I felt a rage unlike anything I had ever experienced before. I felt out of control and helpless."

Maribeth Wilder Doerr, in memory of her children; Andrew, Mark Adam, M.J., Summer Rose and David.

Anger over our loved one's death can sometimes intensify and grow into rage. This uncontrollable feeling can be frightening, and we may feel crazed and panicky. Our heart aches and our mind reels. We have been hurt; our hopes, dreams, and future have been destroyed, changed forever. We want this nightmare to end.

Often our rage and anger hide our feelings of vulnerability. We have been hurt terribly and we're not sure we can endure any more. Our anger and rage have grown more extreme, more powerful, in order to keep further pain away.

Still, we must be careful not to let our anger and rage overpower us. Our feelings of vulnerability need healing. We must begin to slowly release our rage. Sharing our feelings with a trusted friend or support person, or letting them have an outlet in physical exercise may be helpful.

The rage and anger I feel over my loved one's death is real. Even though these feelings wash over me, I will not let them overpower and destroy me. Underneath my anger and rage is a vulnerability that cries out for care.

A New Perspective on Life

"Mom was told in late July that her cancer was too far advanced and she should just go home. One day as I sat next to her, holding her hand as the sun streamed in the window, the realization came to me like a soothing wash of my senses: Of all the things I could possibly be doing in the world right then, nothing was more important than just sitting there, holding this woman's hand and feeding her ice chips. This is what life comes down to in its most basic form. Nothing else really matters. This basic connection speaks to the fullness of what life is about."

Al Honrath, dedicated to the memory of his mother, Rose Kerkvliet Honrath.

Al allowed the illness and death of his mother to affect and enrich his own life. Through this experience he was able to grasp what life meant to him and would mean forever. For Al, new life grew from death; a new perspective was gained.

As we grieve and heal, many of us may also see a new perspective developing from our loved one's death. We may realize it in how we think about our own lives, or how we value our friends or family. Changes in attitude or life choices may signal this newness and show that the cycle of life does continue.

The death of my loved one may give me a new perspective on life. I will be open to these changes.

Differences In How Men
and Women Grieve

*"I was a pallbearer at my grandfather's funeral. When
the service was over, the women hugged each other while
the men stoically shook hands. I wanted a hug, too."*

*Curt Levang, in loving memory of his grandfather,
Lloyd Nungesser.*

The death of a loved one often brings out the
differences in how people grieve. Many women seem
to have an easier time showing their pain. They may
readily cry, hug, and offer sympathy to one another. And
even though men may feel grief just as deeply, they often
continue to take the strong masculine role and show
little outward emotion. Like Curt, they may want
comfort, but expressing this need may seem awkward to
them.

It is important not to judge how others grieve.
Women need to understand that while men may want to
be more open and expressive, some may simply not feel
comfortable with this. Men must also respect their
partner's emotional needs and let them express their
sorrow in their own way.

*I don't have to feel guilty if I have difficulty
showing my emotions. It is okay to express my
grief in whatever way I can.*

Feeling Weak and Aged

"I feel like I've aged ten to twenty years these past few months. After Brennan died I didn't feel I could be carefree and happy anymore. I felt tired, weak and old. I didn't want to be happy and jovial; I wanted to be sad and in mourning."

> Sherokee Ilse, in memory of Brennan William, her beloved son.

The heavy heart, the exhaustion, the work and energy that goes into grieving can make us feel weak and aged. We may walk slower, look older, have little strength, and be tired much of the time. While all these reactions are common, we will need to work hard to counteract them.

Taking vitamins, eating good meals, getting moderate exercise (especially walking), drinking plenty of fluids, staying away from caffeine or alcohol, and getting lots of rest are the best things we can do for ourselves right now. While they cannot totally replenish us either physically or emotionally, they can help.

It is normal to feel weak and aged. To nourish and strengthen myself, I will do two good things for my body and spirit today.

"If Onlys"

"If only I would have made him go to the doctor sooner. If only I had known how sick he was. If only I had been a better daughter. I kept finding reasons to blame myself for what had happened. After awhile this only made me feel worse."

Anna Mallett, in loving memory of her father, Güner Taşkın.

When tragedy strikes, we often feel we need to punish ourselves. Our hurt is so deep that the need to place blame is great, whether that blame is on others or on ourselves. Though it's likely we could not have changed things, even if we believe we could have, there is little we can do now. We need to forgive ourselves and let go of the "if onlys" that haunt us.

I will make a list of my "if onlys." I will cross each one off and tell myself that I need to let go of the guilty feelings and forgive myself. I can put them behind me and move on.

Always a Part of Me

"The phone rang...it was over. My mother had died... That night I talked to her for a long time, perhaps more than I ever had before. She was my last surviving parent, one of the two people who had loved, respected, encouraged, guided and strengthened me and my siblings by their examples. My parents had reflected love for others, respect for differences, appreciation and responsibility for the world around us, acceptance of that which cannot be changed, and recognition that death is simply another part of life, not to be feared.

"I know they aren't gone, for their memories and spirits are with me. They are present in family activities and concerns, encouraging us to help others, enjoy nature's many wonders, and, when pressure builds, their examples provide welcome guidance. No, they aren't gone—thank God!"

Kent Barker, in loving memory of his parents.

Our loved ones never really leave us. We find their spirit and presence in so much of our lives. Their influence walks with us each day, guiding and supporting us. How reassuring it is to know that they will always be a part of our lives.

I can remember how my loved one has influenced my life. They have not left me, but remain inside me forever.

Tears

"Oh that my head were waters, and mine eyes a fountain of tears, that I might weep day and night for the slain of the daughter of my people!"
    Jeremiah 9:1 KJ

Tears can be a sign of love, like freshly picked summer daisies pressed into a mother's waiting hands.

For many of us, the grieving process feels like a raging storm, striking forcefully against our faltering shelter. For others, the storm is a steady downpour, beating ever so incessantly. No one knows when a storm will subside, and the same is true with our tears. But we do know that every storm will pass.

The tears within me are a sign of love. I do not need to hide my love. I will let my tears come.

The Expectations of Others

"I'm so sick of being told 'I should be over it by now.' Why don't they just leave me alone? I don't want to keep pretending I'm fine."

Joyce White, in loving memory of her grandmother, Ella Shea, and her two miscarried babies.

People's expectations about our grieving are often unrealistic. They think we should be doing better by now or that we should be getting on with our life. These expectations can be hurtful and intimidating. Yet we must not forget that their timetable is not ours. We have the right to grieve for as long and as hard as we need.

I do not have to conform to the expectations of others. My grief is my own. I will grieve at my own pace.

Finding Balance In Our Grieving

"As a male, I found it very difficult to strike a balance as to how much I could express my feelings. To say too little was to perpetuate the myth that men don't feel—to say too much seemed to bring my masculinity into question."

Tim Nelson, in loving memory of his daughter, Kathleen.

Many of us struggle with trying to be true to our own feelings while still being concerned about how others perceive us. We don't want to be judged or rejected for how little or how much we grieve. Some of us mourn in public, while others choose to keep grief private. Whatever the case, we must respect our differences. There are no rights or wrongs.

I can accept that I may struggle with finding the right balance for my grieving. I will express my feelings in whatever way I can. I will ask that others accept my way of grieving as I accept theirs.

Disappointment in Careproviders

"My husband Tim and I have found that most people, including our doctor and other professionals, dismissed our grief and concern. I have really anguished alone for the past months. People mean well, but they do not seem to understand."

       Cammy Baer, in loving memory of her miscarried baby.

It's natural to have high expectations of the professionals who surround us, whether they are medical staff, clergy, or mental health professionals. They have been trained in their specialities and we count on them, trusting that they have learned how to handle the emotional, physical, and spiritual aspects of grief. While most of us have good experiences, some of us may feel let down by our careproviders in some way.

The truth of the matter is that there are no simple problems or clear answers where death, dying, and grief are involved. With this in mind, it is understandable that some professionals may have difficulties meeting every individual's special needs. They need our patience and honest communication about how they can best help us. Though this may not be easy in the middle of our grief, we may have to make an attempt.

I will work to let go of any resentment or bitterness I have towards my careproviders. When I am ready, I can share my reactions and suggestions in a letter, a phone call, or during a visit. I will make it a point to also tell them those things which I found helpful.

Isolation

"I am alone.
I want to be alone.
The outside world keeps spinning.
I am dizzy.
I have no need to be a part of the world.
Let me wallow.
Leave me alone."
        Cushla Srour, in loving memory of her children,
Julian and Kieran.

There will be times when we want to be alone, where we can wallow in our pity and despair. For the time being we may want the world to stop so we can get off and hide. Our escape is a means to keep us isolated, if but for the moment. We have little energy or interest in dealing with the people and concerns that surround us.

When I need to be by myself and left alone by others, I will let my needs be known and find a quiet place to retreat.

Caretaking

"We all took Grandpa's death hard. He was our link to the old country, our heritage. Dad, especially, was hardest hit. At the funeral I momentarily lost sight of my Dad. I found him by the church door staring out at the hearse. 'Whatcha doin'?' I asked. 'Saying goodbye to my Dad,' he replied sadly. 'I'll never see him again.' As I choked back the tears, I decided that I had to stuff my own grief; Dad needed me more."

Juliana Ehrman, in memory of her grandfather, Guiseppe Rizzo.

Many of us are natural caretakers. When we see someone hurting we quickly run to alleviate their suffering, putting aside our own feelings and needs. So it is in times of grief; we see someone who is hurting and we readily step forward to comfort them.

Knowing how to give genuine support is a wonderful gift. Those of us with this ability are truly blessed. Lest we forget, however, we need comfort too. If our cup is empty, we will have nothing to give. We must let others replenish our cup.

I can both give and receive the loving care of others. I will let others fill my cup.

Wanting an Ordinary Day

"I just want an ordinary day, one where all I think about are the routine and normal things in life."

Bonnie Fick, in loving memory of her husband, Jack.

There are times when we crave a normal life, one where the little things are the important things; noticing the birds, the clouds, making dinner, watching a television show, calling a friend or relative just to chat.

We need days like this, days where we do not have to think or feel, and we can just be.

Today I will let myself be, without thinking or feeling anything too deeply. I will find an ordinary activity and enjoy it.

Support Groups

"When the support group meeting ended, my grief was just as heavy, but emotionally I felt like I could fly. I now knew that I wasn't crazy, just mourning, and I began to look forward to my weekly 'release.'"

Laure Janus, in loving memory of her mother.

Support groups may be a lifeline for many of us after the death of our loved one. While they cannot magically take our pain away, the moral support we gain can validate our feelings and offer us comfort and consulation.

The prevalence of support groups may partly be a result of the distance that separates many families today. Our natural family support systems may not be large or very accessible, and support groups can offer a safe, nonthreatening place to share our emotions and concerns.

Not all of us can or do seek support from a group. We may feel we are private, quiet, or independent people who have difficulty in groups, or we may think that a group will not meet our needs. Yet at some point or another, if we cannot find the outlet for our grief that will help us, we may wish to visit a group if one is near. At least we will meet others who have been through what we have.

By attending a support group I can meet other people who have walked a similar path, and who can share my grief. I will allow myself to seek support from others during those inevitable times when I am in need of comfort and understanding.

Being Unable to Function Normally

"My Dad's death was very trying. One morning I went out, started up the car, and backed out only to hear a very loud crash. My initial thought was that one of my daughters had left her bike behind the car. When I glanced in the rearview mirror, I was shocked to see that I hadn't opened the garage door! I was so out of step with life that I didn't realize what I was doing."

Suzanne Bangert, in loving memory of her father, Robert Tenner.

For many, the shock of a loved one's death can temporarily interrupt normal functioning. Moving about like wooden soldiers, we may lift our arms and legs mechanically, as if to some distant drummer's beat. Day to day living can be difficult, for we may have trouble concentrating, carrying on conversations, completing simple tasks, or even listening to others. Thoughts may ramble, and we may wonder whether or not we have replied to a question we've been asked or if we've somehow repeated ourselves. We may even misplace the car keys and find them next to the toothpaste in the medicine cabinet!

The sensation of being disconnected from our bodies can make life difficult. As the shock diminishes, we will regain control.

For now, my body may not function as it usually does. I will attempt to be patient with myself and accept my limitations.

Ways to Pray

"Intensity seems to
Estrange
Or perhaps it
Just wearies
Like too much
Wind or
Sun or
Rain—
If I could not Pray
I would die of Exposure."

Ellen Olinger, in loving memory of her father, Harold A. Borgh.

In the midst of our intense grief we may find that prayer gives us comfort and solace. For some, like Ellen, prayer is a virtual lifeline, providing the stability we desperately require. While we can rely on the short prayers of childhood, we can also engage in simple conversations, like those we have with valued friends. A conversation with God can happen most anywhere; while getting dressed, taking a short walk, driving in the car, waiting for an appointment, or having that last cup of coffee at the end of a meal. Our prayers—simple or formal—are a means of communicating.

I can take time today to share my thoughts with God. Whether I use formal or simple prayers, they can provide me with comfort and solace.

Untitled

by Patti Fochi, in memory of her son, Justin.

The deafening silence begins again
I start to tremble
I want to run, to hide
   But there is no place to go
This silence follows me

My own heartbeat sounds like
   ten thousand drums
Each beat crashes in my brain
I close my eyes...
         but I still see
            emptiness

I still feel...
        the emptiness

I search my soul for a refuge
   and I find only confusion
Confusion screaming at me
   falling down around me
       in silence

There is no place to run
I cannot hide from this reality
I cannot deny the pain in my heart
The emptiness pulls me, draws me into
   this deafening silence.

The Uneven Path

Settling Differences

"Many things, small irritations and upsets, had existed between my mother and I for some time. As her death was impending, we both knew this was 'it' for us. After a couple weeks together, with me helping Dad provide twenty-four hour care for her, Mom and I made our peace with one another. I feel grateful for the quiet time we had to work through our differences."

Al Honrath, in loving memory of his mother, Rose Kerkvliet Honrath.

Life is never quite like a storybook. Having a strained relationship prior to our loved one's death is not all that uncommon. Thankfully, some of us had an opportunity to work out our differences and, together, many of us were able to find peace.

Yet for others, that time for peace never presented itself. We are left haunted by the ill feelings and unfinished sentences. It is sad and disturbing to think that forgiveness never came. Carrying such a burden is difficult.

Though they have died, we can make amends to our loved one. By setting aside some quiet time, we can say our peace, lay aside our differences, and offer forgiveness. We can let the things that were left unsaid come into the open and purge them from our minds and hearts.

I can settle the differences and strained relationship I had with my loved one. I will find some quiet time to say my peace and to both offer and ask for forgiveness.

Making Good Choices

"Against the well-meaning advice of others, we took a trip soon after my son and my father died. We went away for the holidays. Not being at home with our memories during that period made it easier.

"It was the best thing we could have done, for it gave us time to find our individual strengths, and it helped us face what had happened. In addition, we grew so much stronger physically, mentally and emotionally."

Mayrse Wilde, in memory of her son, Ricky-Adrian, and her father, Adrien.

We are likely to be given well-meaning advice in hopes that it will lessen our pain and speed up our recovery. Yet others do not know us as well as we do. If we need a vacation, a break in tradition, or a time away, we must trust ourselves and do what we need to do. It may be hard to attend family functions such as picnics, weddings, family reunions, or baptisms. Maybe attending special church services or other social gatherings is especially painful, too.

As hard as it is for others to understand why we can't participate in these events or why we don't follow their advice, it is up to us to determine what is best for us. We can explain our feelings and needs and ask for support. Our first obligation is to take care of ourselves.

I am a capable person who knows deep down inside what is best for me. If I need a getaway or to decline an invitation, I can do so gracefully. I will trust my judgment and try to make decisions based on what I need, not what others think will be the best for me.

Validity of Loss

"I finally feel like I have permission to grieve. My sense of pain and loss is valid!"

Sonja Fowler, in loving memory of Baby Fowler, miscarried at eight weeks.

All of us need others who genuinely understand us. This is especially true when we are in pain. It is natural to want to be surrounded by understanding people who know our kind of pain and will allow us to have it. Our society often tells us that we shouldn't feel so badly, or that we should be over our grief by a particular point in time. Sometimes we may even get the feeling that we don't have the right to be in pain.

Sonja felt that after three years of crying and grieving alone, she wanted someone to help her pretend it never happened, so she could stop crying. The pressures she felt—from her family, community, and her own emotions—made her feel like she was "sick" to dwell on her grief.

Many of us try to go about our lives while we are still wounded, feeling like Sonja. Yet it might be helpful to face the loss, experience the pain, and cherish the memories.

My sense of pain and loss is valid. I have a right to my pain, sadness, joy, confusion; my feelings. I will find others to support this important message.

The Uneven Path

When Others Seem to Have Forgotten

"Sometimes I feel as if everyone else has forgotten. I wonder if I'll get any cards on Mother's Day, or the anniversary. I wonder if they even remember I had a baby."

Kimberly D. Lay, in loving memory of her precious daughter, Lucinda.

After a few months, people often stop talking about what has happened to us and seem to assume we are mostly "over it." They may ask the universal yet meaningless question, "How are you?" It's not difficult to guess the answer they hope to hear, which is "Fine." It seems that few people really wish to share in our remembering for as long as we would like. Family members and friends may not think to call us or send flowers or a card on those special holidays and anniversaries. Their lives seem to have gone on. Maybe they are trying to tell us to go on with ours, too.

Most people are not hurtful by nature. They are probably trying to protect us and themselves from the pain because they're not sure how to help any longer. What they may not realize is that we need cards, calls, and quiet chats, especially as we move towards holidays and anniversaries. Remembering is important. Sharing our memories with someone who cares and is willing to try to understand us helps in our healing. As hard as it is to ask for help, there may be times when we have to in order to get the support we need and deserve.

When support has dropped off, but my needs have not, I will call someone to be with me. I will let them know that remembering is important to my healing, and that I need to share my memories and pain with someone who is special to me.

Forgiving Ourselves

"I'm sorry for so many things; for what my son went through, for how much he suffered in body and heart. It wasn't right, it wasn't fair! If I could have taken his place, I would have."

Deanna Gorzynski, in loving memory of her firstborn son, Gregory.

How hurt we can feel because of all the things we weren't able to fix or undo for our loved one. The "I'm sorrys" echo endlessly in our heart and we feel disappointed and self-critical. We may feel guilty for being alive and not having made things better.

While it may not be easy to forgive ourselves and let go of our regrets, we can work towards this. By judging ourselves harshly we may reject hope and healing. We need to let go of the past. We need to acknowledge our regrets and move on.

I am truly sorry for the things I could or should have done. I will stop judging myself. I will seek forgiveness and move forward.

Giving and Receiving Love

"I'd awaken at night—sometimes to labored breathing, sometimes to barely a breath at all. A gentle hand on his seemed to help in either case. I would wash his body and feed him with food and the Spirit. Then he died. Now I am filled with this overabundant intimate love that only he could receive the way it is meant to be given...but he's gone, and I have no one to take my love."

    C. Renee Anderson, in loving memory of her husband, Keith.

With the death of our loved one, many of us may feel that our ability to give and receive love has been torn from us forever. The closeness and intimacy we once shared tenderly and freely may have no real outlet now, and our heart aches. We feel robbed and cheated. It is natural for us to miss our loved one and long to love again.

My loved one's death has left we with no one to take my love the way they received it. I miss my loved one and our special relationship. I can acknowledge that I long to give and receive love again.

Alive in Our Hearts

"As the days go by, they tell me I will get better and not hurt so much. This is most likely true, but this does not mean my love or memory of my daughter will be less. Oh, no! I will always keep her alive in my heart and tell people that I have four children."

Becky Geppert, in memory of her daughter, Rebecca Joy, always walking in her heart.

Healing and getting better does not mean forgetting or loving any less. And yet, others may expect us to move on quickly, often in a few weeks' time. They appear to be telling us to stop thinking about our loved one and to reinvest in the living. What they may not understand is that in order to work towards healing, we need to remember, not forget, our loved ones.

It is important to include our loved one's memory in our lives. Just because they died does not mean they are no longer a part of our family. When a mother dies, we don't pretend she didn't exist. We acknowledge her as our mother and carry her memories and specialness inside of us, now and forever. We still love her. We can't help but love her. And so it is for any special person who dies.

I never have to fear that I must stop loving or remembering my loved one. I will always save a place for them in my heart and in my life.

Looking Back On Humorous Moments

"At Mom's funeral we found my son, Tommy, only five, jumping off the table in the foyer of the funeral home. He'd been licking shut all the memorial cards that hadn't been used! And, my daughter, Megan, was discovered in a basket of roses—she'd slipped trying to smell each and every one. Now, after some time has passed, I can laugh about these things. At the time, though, I just couldn't."

Mary Laing Kingston, in loving memory of her mother, who died at home after an extended illness.

In the early weeks and months following our loved one's death, humor may not have had a place in our life. That is understandable. But now, after some time has passed, we may be able to look back and recall some humorous moments just as Mary did.

By remembering these times and actually laughing about them, we may be able to build some positive memories of our loved one's last weeks and days. Often, our memories from this time are painful and heartbreaking. Recalling some of the comical or less serious times may help lift our spirits and let us feel just a bit better.

Now that time has passed, I can think about some of the funny things that happened near the time of my loved one's death. I will use these humorous moments to build some positive memories and lift my spirits a bit.

Suppressing Our Tears

"There are times when the grief explodes inside me... A smell, a sound, a holiday...anything can trigger it. It may only last a few seconds, or it can last for hours. I have learned to let myself cry, think, and feel, and to go with the feelings for however long it takes to work through the grief."

Jill Cerulli

Sadly, many of us have been taught to suppress our tears. The stern words, "Big boys don't cry" is a message many men have heard. Many of us have come to believe that tears and masculinity are like oil and vinegar—they just don't mix. And although many women have been taught that it's okay to express emotions, this is only tolerated for a limited time. Before long an inner voice may begin to echo, "Don't whine—you've cried long enough."

Thankfully, Jill has learned to let herself cry. She sees crying as a valid way of grieving, and has come to believe that it is futile to deny this very human act. Crying is not a sign of weakness; tears demonstrate the depth of our love and our sorrow. They are the outward display of our internal pain; a valid emotion, that begs for release.

I will release my tears. I will not pent them up and hide them away. I will let the world see how deeply I cared.

Creating Balance

"I feel so out of balance, overloaded with this heavy burden of grief. It's as if a hurricane relentlessly dashes my body and soul upon the hard shore."

Anonymous

We may all be able to relate to the feelings of being out of control and out of balance, especially after our lives have drastically changed. We are easily frustrated, overwhelmed and out of focus. Decisions are difficult, we crack easily and at times it may feel as if we are drowning.

We may not be able to totally stop the hurricane at this point, but we may be able to do little things in our daily living to provide some positive balance. Pleasant thoughts, nostalgic memories, and adding brightness and inspiration to our lives can bring momentary happiness. Thus we can build strength and renew our spirits, if but a few moments at a time.

I can paint the walls of my mind with beautiful pictures and pleasant thoughts. I can reflect on past memories and inspirations that have brought me joy.

Facing the Pain

"Go through your pain, through the center of it. Do not try to run around it, or give in to it. Go through it.
"Go through the center of your joy. Let yourself rejoice in what you are doing. Rejoice to the fullest."
    *from **Christian Wholeness: Spiritual Growth for Today**, by Jesse Trotter, in loving memory of his son, John.*

Too many of us try to avoid or give in to the pain that life and death presents. We may not entirely embrace the joy in life, either. In order for us to live life fully and heal from our losses, we can be challenged to face the pain, sorrow, and the joy straight on. We can dare ourselves to go through them, even though we may be anxious and fearful. We can trust in the wholeness of our God, our faith, and ourselves.

Today I can go straight through my pain, facing it squarely. I can also embrace the joy that is still in my life.

The Power of Fear

"One of my greatest fears was that one day I would lose control and go completely insane."

Phyllis DeBella, in loving memory of her son, Jesse, her daughter, Katie, and her father.

Fear is a powerful emotional and physical response to change. When we are grieving, many fears arise. We fear that we will lose control. We fear we will forget, thus turning our loved one's life into something unimportant to us and to others. And we fear we won't be able to forget our pain and go on with life. We may also fear that another crisis will happen to us or someone we love.

Facing a fear may be easier said than done. Whether based on fantasy or reality, fear is real. We may find it helpful to try to clarify what our fears are, to say them out loud. We may also wish to share them with someone who may be able to help us understand and deal with them.

I will attempt to face a fear today. I can write it down or share it with someone I trust. With this start, I can bring a fear from inside of me out into the open.

Dreams That Bring Peace

"I never believed that I would recover from the images of my father's horrible death. Then one night, several months after he died, I dreamt of him well; he was with me in a restaurant in the town where I grew up. In my dream he said, 'It's not important how I left...let go of it. I'm fine now. That's all that matters.' That dream helped my healing."

Donna Damico Mayer, in memory of her father, Joseph Damico.

Many of us have disturbing visions after our loved one has died. The part that haunts us plays over and over in our minds. We may feel badly for our loved one, that their life was cut so short. We may wonder if they left this world in pain, and whether their pain has continued. We may even try to imagine their last moments, and fear they were frightened or angry that they were dying.

Over and over again, people have described dreams, feelings, and strong sensations that help them believe their loved one is now experiencing peace and joy. When we gain this insight, we can feel a sense of reassurance about our loved one, and perhaps stop worrying and wondering about the last moments of their life and their eternal peace.

I will allow myself to believe that my loved one is now at peace, not in pain or angry, but content. I will listen for this message and seek peace about their death.

The Continuing Struggle

"Almost four months have passed. It seems like years, but we are taking one day at a time. I have some very hard days and some good ones."

Susan and Fred Stewart, in loving memory of their son, Travis Fred.

The good days may sneak in among the bad. But even the hard days aren't all bad; there are moments of light and hope, and slowly we can begin to dream again.

It's an uphill struggle, one that requires faith, trust, and love. We may feel as if we've been on this journey for an eternity, and yet at other times it seems it has just begun. The ups and downs will not be predictable nor controllable. We are going somewhere we have never been before. It won't be easy, but it will be possible.

In my continuing struggle I will use my faith to seek trust, understanding, and hope for tomorrow.

Feeling Vulnerable

*"There are many times when my heart stops; at the doctor's office, when the kids get hurt, or if an unusual symptom crops up that I worry could be cancerous or fatal. I always expect the worst, because I know that the worst **does** happen. I feel so vulnerable, defenseless, and out of control."*

> *Bonnie Fick, in loving memory of her husband Jack, her son, Tommy, and her dad, Bob Mohler.*

We may find ourselves worrying about ourselves and others, fearing or expecting that something bad will happen again. Since we have been one of the statistics, we no longer find comfort in numbers, or in reassurances that we can stop worrying because we've had our fair share of pain.

Though it may not always seem rational, it is natural for survivors of tragedies to feel especially vulnerable and defenseless. We know that bad things happen to good people, and that there are no guarantees in life. Yet we still want them.

Today I can live with the vulnerable feelings I have. I can let go of the need to control everything and seek a balance where possible.

Emptiness

"An aching heart,
tired and swollen eyes,
a heavy chest
all weighed down
by pure emptiness."

*from **The Anguish of Loss** by Julie Fritsch, in loving memory of her son, Justin.*

When a major branch breaks off a tree, the tree becomes traumatized and often goes into a state of distress. It may wilt, its leaves may turn brown and fall. Some of the roots may die, and other parts of the tree may be affected as well.

In much the same way, the emptiness we feel when a loved one dies can affect us physically. Difficulty breathing, a heavy chest, and swollen eyes are all natural responses following a loved one's death. They are a result of the trauma and stress we are under. This emptiness won't always overwhelm us with such intense physical reactions, but our hearts and minds will always hold a place open for this special person.

I will accept the tears and physically wrenching reactions I have to my loved one's death. It is right for the empty and aching feelings to be inside my heart now. I will have hope that tomorrow or next week it won't feel so intense. I will share my sorrow with someone who can allow me to miss my loved one.

Goodbyes

"That last hug...
That last goodbye
I'll treasure them always.

He wouldn't have wanted to live
in that broken body."
        Barbara Carnes, in memory of her father,
Francis E. Sly.

If we had the chance to say goodbye to our loved one, we cherish those bittersweet moments together. Undoubtedly, our parting thoughts and feelings may be among the most poignant and remarkable moments in our life. They are both bitter and so very sweet and tender; a treasure of undeniable value.

Not everyone is able to say their goodbyes face to face. Still, we can create our own special parting as we say goodbye in other ways. We can write a letter to our loved one, say farewell at a private place we shared, or visit the cemetery to express some parting thoughts. Loving and tender, these actions can be a very valued goodbye, no matter when they take place.

I will treasure my last goodbye to my loved one. Created or lived, our parting was a very special, personal farewell.

Reinvesting in Life

*"I can live for today instead of yesterday. I can love again because I know now that moving on does not mean leaving my love for Tom behind. I don't feel guilty for feeling good. I carry Tom's love with me always, which helps me to accept, embrace, and **live** this new life."*

Jane Kaysen McDowell, in memory of her husband, soulmate, and friend, Thomas Matthew.

When clouds part and the sun shines through, our outlook on life can improve. We need not feel guilty for enjoying the day or looking forward to an activity off in the future. Instead we need to seize the moment and reinvest in living for today. We can enjoy the sun and blue sky whenever they are present in our lives.

I will enjoy a happy thought today. I can make plans for something in the future, even if it is tomorrow. It is good to reinvest in living.

Addictive Behaviors

"The greatest positive step I took was to stop drinking alcohol. It changed my perspective about living and made sleeping much easier."

Alan E. Wulzen, in loving memory of his wife, Elisabeth Roberts, and daughter, Catherine Wulzen, who both died in childbirth.

The death of our loved one can badly damage our sense of worth. We can usually find so many things to blame ourselves for or to find fault with. Why couldn't we keep them from dying? Why weren't we there to protect them? We may feel inadequate, and many of us try to cover up our feelings of worthlessness by turning to drugs, alcohol, or other addictive behaviors. Yet hiding from our pain won't help us feel better about ourselves. Alan found that out. In order to feel good, we need to face our insecurities and tackle them head on. We must stop running away from ourselves and our pain.

Turning to drugs, alcohol or other addictive behaviors will not make me feel better. I can face the insecure feelings I have, and not run away.

Fitting In Socially

"Trying to fit in is a real dilemma for me. I don't feel all that comfortable with our old bridge club—they're married couples. The singles groups are not much better. Most events seem to focus on young adults, and I have family responsibilities to contend with. What am I—married or single? Where do I fit in now?"

Anonymous

For many of us, knowing what group we fit in with or what label to call ourselves can cause some discomfort after our loved one dies. Whether our partner, parent, child, sibling, or fiance died, the issue remains the same. How do we maintain our loved one's memory and yet function with the labels and categories? Where do we fit in? Facing grandparent's day at school, having to check off single or married on forms, or being asked how many children we have can all be distressing. These seemingly small issues can be confusing and hurtful for us.

Finding the right niche and fitting in again may be a matter of trial and error. Relying on an understanding friend to support our choices and help us think about our dilemma may help ease the burden and lower our stress.

At times it is a challenge for me to find a way to fit in again. I can learn to adjust no matter the group or label.

Their Suffering Has Ended

"What is much too real for me is the large lump of memories I carry in my heart of all the pain and sickness that were so much a part of over half of my son's life. And when those memories come back, I am very glad that he is free from that part of the human experience. There's just no way I can make any of that make sense."

Dan J. Henderson, in loving memory of his only child, Nathan.

Like Dan, we may feel glad that the illness or difficulties that our loved one suffered are now over, finally and forever. Having had to witness them in torment or distress saddened us, and might have left us feeling somewhat guilty and anxious. Though we were powerless to help them, we felt their pain; we cried when they cried and bled when they bled. While their pain has ended, ours has just begun. They have been set free.

I can feel glad that my loved one's suffering has ended. I am thankful that they have been set free.

Uncertain of the Future

"The magnitude of the loss of our daughter is devastating. My husband and I feel lost and alone. Our whole family is miserable, and as of today I wonder what the future is without our little girl."

Karen Bell, in loving memory of her daughter, Becky.

A great many of us worry about the future, even long after our loved one's death. It is so uncertain and confusing for us. What we had expected and planned for has vanished. We want and need some reassurances; we want to know what lies ahead. The future has shattered like broken glass, and we want to know how to go on.

The future I had dreamt and planned seems to have vanished. I will look for reassurances in those things that have given me strength in the past.

Cultural and Religious Differences

"A good friend told me that some Native Americans believe the cedar tree has healing powers. She made me a 'burden basket' of cedar boughs. Whenever I am troubled I write down my sorrows and put them in the burden basket. This brings me comfort and relief."
Anonymous

Every culture and religion has special beliefs, ceremonies, and traditions meant to foster healing. Various Christian faiths have an All Saints Day to commemorate those who have died, while the Jewish faith offers a Yorseit to celebrate and remember the annual anniversary of departed relatives and friends. While we may find comfort in the traditions with which we were raised, we may also find that those of other faiths hold special meaning for us.

We may want to explore various beliefs and traditions, and embrace those in which we find solace. This new understanding lets us reach out to other groups and faiths, having found common threads of grief.

I can explore the traditions and beliefs of other faiths as well as my own, and find comfort in those which have special meaning to me. I can use my new understanding of other cultures and religions to find the common threads which bind us together in our grieving.

Feeling Deserted By Our Loved One

"I don't feel like a survivor. I feel left behind."
    Helen Bevington, in memory of her husband.

It hurts to feel abandoned or deserted by our loved one. We wanted to be with them forever; at least that's what we planned. Continuing on without them is disappointing, lonely, and frustrating.

No one wants to be the one left behind. But like it or not, we can't change places with our loved one. They are gone and we can't bring them back. We are the survivors. We must go on, if only to live the life they couldn't.

I feel hurt that I've been left behind. Still, I know I can't change places with my loved one. I will make the most of the life I have.

Feeling Distant from God

"Here I am, God... Where are You?
   Deep down in my heart I know You
   Are there, but I don't feel
   Your presence.
      I have been hurt so deeply...
      I feel betrayed, angry,
      broken in pieces."
         Anne Byrnes, in loving memory of her son,
Jimmy.

In the throes of our pain and sorrow, God may sometimes seem distant and removed. The great weight of our emotions—anger, confusion, disappointment, and despair—may distort our image of God, and we may not see Him positively. We may sense that He is too far-away, too distant, both physically and emotionally, to be of any real help.

For now, we can let God meet us where we are—in the midst of our doubts, uncertainties, and feelings of estrangement. We must be patient during these times. As our feelings calm, we may find that God has been waiting for us all along.

I can be patient with the feelings and questions I have about God. I trust that even in those times when He seems far, He is near.

Low Self-Esteem

"Plummeted to rock bottom, I felt like an ant trying to swim across a swimming pool and never making progress. The water was black, and there was no light near the pool. Now I can't even swim to save myself. I feel worthless."

Cushla Srour, in loving memory of her children, Julian and Kieran.

Feeling worthless, incapable, and inadequate are some of the feelings that may plague us in the months following our loss. Our low self-esteem can affect our outlook on life and our interactions with others, not to mention how we feel about ourselves. Even simple tasks can intimidate us when we doubt ourselves. This temporary condition can make it difficult to function at times.

Though we need not run away from these feelings, we may want to seek some sunshine and light to brighten our mood. A walk and some fresh air, or an enjoyable activity may lift our spirits.

When I am feeling low and worthless, I will find some sunshine in my day. I need only start small.

For Whom Am I Grieving?

"When my mom died I felt overwhelmed with grief and despair. It was such a vivid reminder; I had been there before. I often found myself thinking of my babies and my grandfather, all of whom had died previously. I was confused at times, wondering for whom I was grieving."

    Sherokee Ilse, in loving memory of her mother and her grandfather.

    A death, any death, often leads us to recall previous losses, and the raw feelings of those times return. When we experience a new loss in our lives we are also likely to find our past grief resurfacing. We are no longer crying only for this new loss; we also feel heavy-hearted about the other special people in our lives who have died.

    Reliving older grief at the time of a new crisis is very natural, yet it can be disturbing. We may not realize we are experiencing both kinds of grief. The pressure to be done with past losses can confuse us, especially when it arises unexpectedly during a new tragedy. We need not let this overwhelm us, but rather by incorporating our prior experiences, they may actually help us weather this new loss. Reliving past losses through new losses is the basis of the grieving process; thus it is a path to healing.

If I find myself remembering the pain of a previous loss, I will allow it to surface. These feelings and memories are a part of the continuous process of grieving and healing.

Private Grief

"The shower and the car ride to and from work became the only places I allowed myself to feel. The tears were easily washed away in the shower and the angry words were swallowed up in the empty car. Best of all, no one was the wiser."

> *Tim Nelson, in loving memory of his daughter, Kathleen.*

There may be times when we would rather grieve alone. We may find comfort in solitude and the freedom to express ourselves however we need to. We may cry while showering, taking long walks, driving in the car, or late at night while others are asleep. By reserving a private time and place for ourselves we may find it easier to make it through the day. It may be reassuring to know we will have this time alone.

I can find a special time and place to grieve. The solitude of this private time helps me make it through the day.

Avoidance by Friends and Family

"When a person is born, we rejoice. When they are married, we celebrate. When they die, we pretend nothing happened."
   Margaret Mead

As a society we seem to be good at avoiding what we perceive as the negative side of life: death and grief. Our pursuit of happiness and the pleasures in life overshadow those painful but important losses in our lives. Births, weddings, deaths, and funerals are all significant events in a family's life. The happy occasions will be relived for years through pictures and memories. But more often than not, the funerals and lives of those who have died will be tucked away in an attic and rarely discussed openly.

While some families do pass on memories of the funeral and stories of their loved ones who have died, many have a hard time talking about them, especially in the early months. Friends and co-workers may be especially likely to avoid the subject, and may even act as if nothing has happened. Their actions may be motivated by their own discomfort at not knowing what to say, or because they don't want to cause us more pain. All of this may make it difficult to get the support we need over time. We may have to work hard at seeking support as we mourn our loss.

I will try to be understanding when people avoid the subject of my love one's death and the grief I am experiencing. Even if they act as if nothing has happened, I will follow the path I must take and seek support as I need it.

Choices of Attitudes

"You cannot prevent the birds of sorrow from flying overhead, but you can prevent them from building nests in your hair."
Chinese Proverb

Sorrow eventually comes to all of us. We each have our false sense of immortality threatened when a loved one dies; our protective bubble has burst. The death of our loved one is a major crisis in our lives; it has brought sorrow and heartache.

Although we could not prevent our loved one's death, we do have choices about how we handle this tragedy. We can have a positive attitude, face our grief, and try to keep the nests of sorrow from building inside us; we don't have to allow ourselves to die emotionally and spiritually. This is our choice and our challenge.

Although I agonize over my loss, I can make choices about my attitude. I can survive this and grow if I believe, trust, and have faith.

Loss and Gain

"Vernon's death came suddenly—too soon for all of us. We were not ready to say goodbye. As we murmured words of hope and consolation to one another we knew that someone irreplaceable among us was gone. We are less. But we are more, too, because of Vernon and what he brought to us. And as we pray we ask that all the ways Vernon was a good and decent man will continue to live in our courage and in our conscience."

The staff and volunteers of Interfaith Outreach and Community Partners, in memory of Vernon Anderson, co-worker and friend.

There is a certain "less and more" quality to death. We are less because we have lost a unique person in our life. They cannot be replaced; they are gone forever. Our world is empty where they once stood.

Still, we are more. We are more because our loved one gave much to our life, perhaps by making it better, more beautiful or more joyful. Though they are gone, their spirit lives on in us; their presence is still filling our world.

The death of my loved one is both a "more" and a "less." I am less because they are gone, but I am more because of what they have given. I will let their spirit live on in me.

The Senselessness of Death

"When people tell me 'the universe is random,' it doesn't help. Not when I am trying to make sense of a senseless loss."

Kathryn M. Sherman, in memory of her miscarriage.

The senselessness of death, loss, and grief may overwhelm us at times. The anguish we feel cannot be explained away by people who offer reasons why this tragedy happened to us, and why it happened when it did. The truth is that there may be no reason which we can comprehend. It happened. For now, we need to find a way to go on. While it is not fair, we do not have the power to rewrite the story. We can only go on from here.

Though this senseless death overpowers me at times, I do not need to find a valid reason why it happened. I can slowly work on accepting reality and go on from here.

Coping Strategies

"I felt so empty and sad when Ellen died. I knew I had to find a way to cope and go on. It felt like there was an invisible door in front of me, and if I could somehow get through it, everything would be okay—I could manage."

Cathy Schmidt, in loving memory of her friend and co-worker, F. Ellen Walz.

Unfortunately, no one knows the best or "right" way to cope with the death of a loved one. Each of us approaches our grief with different strengths and resources. Finding our own pathway, our "invisible door," is a process. While others may offer suggestions from their own experience, we may need to depend on the coping strategies that have worked for us in the past. Having overcome previous difficulties or stressful situations can give us the knowledge and hope we need to survive.

I can remember other troubled or difficult times that I have survived. I will use these resources to help me cope. I will rejoice with every small victory.

Forever Changed

"She changed my life forever,
and I will never be the same.
Some say for the better.
Oh, I just want to hear my baby's name."
        Kevin Kidnie, in loving memory of Erin Marie.

As hard as it might be to believe at first, we are forever changed when someone we love dies. We can no longer call them on the phone, touch them, share a story with them, or build our future with them. We miss them. Yet somehow we go on, eventually seeking some normalcy in our lives. Even though much of life around us does seem to continue as before, we still long for their presence; the sound of their name, their voice, and the validation that they were real and that they are remembered.

I know that life has changed significantly since my loved one's death. I can work towards rebuilding my life. But it is okay for me to still want to hear their name spoken and to miss them for all that was, and all that could have been.

In Memoriam
by LaDonna Hoy

Our loved ones...
  are the saints among us ...
    whose memory we share...
      whose absence we mourn...
        whose new life we celebrate.

Young...old...just beginning life...
  and in the prime of life
    when they left us,
They had spouses...and children
    to love...
boyfriends...and grandchildren...
    they adored...
  dreams...hopes...plans...

Caught up in a greater plan, they rest now in the silent
  heart of God...
and in a parting act of trust, leave the ones they love to
  us...

We remember...We mourn...We celebrate...We keep
  their love alive...as we journey on our way

The Uneven Path

Engulfed in Anger

"Anger entered my life one day like a giant beast clutching me in its paws. Day after day I awoke angry. I was angry throughout each day, and I went to bed at night angry."

Betty Jane Spencer, in memory of her four murdered sons.

Anger can and does engulf many of us as we grieve. There can be so many things to feel angry about, and so many people to be angry with.

It is normal to feel angry. Still, many of us find it difficult to admit we're angry, and others tend to ignore it, thinking it will go away on its own. It is important for us to recognize and come to terms with our anger. Hiding or suppressing it only leads to other problems. Admitting that we are angry or upset and taking steps to deal with these feelings will help us move on in our grieving.

I have a right to feel angry now. I will admit when I am angry and work to release it by exercising vigorously, hitting a pillow, or some other safe means.

Healing Through Sharing Ourselves

"You know you are healing when you are able to comfort or console someone else. Your heart understands and breaks for their loss, even though you may never have met before. You realize you know each other in the most intimate ways."

Jane Kaysen McDowell, in memory of her husband, soulmate, and friend, Thomas Matthew.

Helping someone else who is in pain can bring a rewarding feeling. Our compassion for others aids them in feeling less alone and opens our heart to the healing that follows. To give is to receive, and to reach out is to care. To share of ourselves means we have the energy and strength to move out of our own pain and sorrow. This is an important stepping stone on the path to healing.

I will give of myself today. I will offer comfort to a child, a friend, a relative, or an acquaintance who is hurting and needs my support.

Visiting the Cemetery

"I went to the cemetery a few weeks ago. Jesse's marker was there. When I saw his name on it I felt so much grief that it was like he had just died. I cried so hard I could hardly breathe."

Susan Price, in memory of her son, Jesse Lee.

Visiting the cemetery can be a very traumatic experience for some of us. It may feel like a foreign and unfamiliar place where the reality of our loved one's death becomes even more overwhelming. We may feel disturbed when we are there, and never quite comfortable. Our visits may be infrequent. Or, we may find peace at the gravesite and visit it regularly. Although it may not always be easy, we may welcome the solitude and find solace and comfort from being close to our loved one.

It is important that each of us follow our own heart when it comes to visiting the gravesite or special place of our loved one. Focusing on what we need to feel connected with our loved one may be best.

I will listen to my heart and make my own decision about visiting the cemetery. I trust that I know what brings me comfort.

Relieving Sadness

"I learned to do what it takes to relieve my sadness. I made a memory book, wrote poems, wrote Caleb a letter telling him how much I loved him, and did whatever else that helped me feel better."

Judy Bierbower, in memory of her son, Caleb.

Each of us needs to find ways to relieve our own sadness. We can look within ourselves to find these healing tools and ask others for their thoughts. Judy was able to help herself feel better, even if it meant letting herself cry. We can lift our heads up, listen to our hearts, and do what we feel is helpful for the moment.

I will think of two or three things that may relieve my sadness today. I will start working on at least one of them.

Social Dilemmas

"I had friends who said, 'Call me if there is anything I can do.' They didn't come over again, never invited us out, and I could not get up the nerve to call them. Then, I had other friends who invited us to lunch, baby showers and parties. I felt awkward, as if they were pressuring us to 'buck up,' 'snap out of it,' and 'get back into life.'"

Bonnie Fick, in loving memory of her son, Tommy.

Dilemmas can arise as friends and relatives struggle with how to help us. They may wonder when and if they should begin to include us again in gatherings and special occasions. They may sit back and wait for our requests for help, offer to help yet not make accepting it easy, or invite us often, letting us decide. We need to use our own judgment about attending events or asking for help, and trust that we will not be judged harshly if we decline.

Our family and friends are in a difficult spot while we are mourning. They can't read our minds, and they aren't sure how or when to help. We will have to let them know, and be open about our needs. They will only be able to help us if we're honest with them.

I will attempt to be open and honest with people about my personal and social needs.

Replaying the Tragedy

"I know it was morbid of me to keep going over the details of her death, but for some reason I had to do that. Eventually, I think it helped me get used to the idea, and I did feel somewhat better."

Linda Hall Whitman, in loving memory of her mother.

Replaying the events over and over in our minds is a common thing to do. We may find ourselves repeating the details to everyone, sometimes even the same people. We probably do have a need to repeat the story, even though it is painful. We may need to keep going over the details because it is something we still have trouble believing. This repetition allows us to eventually accept what has happened, and also help us deal with our shock.

Telling the story is a part of the healing process. The more we talk about it, the more details we remember, and so do others. We can then store these recollections away for some later day when we might need them.

When I repeat the story over and over I will remember that I am on the road to healing. It's okay to replay events in my mind.

Death as an Integral Part of Life

"He died at home, unexpectedly. I just happened to be there. It was the first time I saw death happen. It felt like my father's last and greatest gift to me. It was easier to see death than to hear about it afterward. I realized it's not LIFE and DEATH. It's birth, morning and evening, graduation and marriage, and death. Death is an integral part of life, not a separate event. The illness was awful, but death wasn't. It was peaceful and natural, simple and momentous at the same time. In my father's case, it was an okay kind of hurt. It was his time. It relieved suffering."

Margery Peterson, in loving memory of her father, Walter Kaul.

While the death of our loved one is painful to us, it may be something we can come to accept. We may have sensed the peace that surrounded them in death and we may want to remind ourselves that their troubles and suffering are over. Now, we are the ones who are left to deal with their death and live on.

Death is an important and inevitable part of life. As we struggle with our journey of 'going on,' we will find that life is indeed morning and evening, an ongoing process of which death is a part. Life and death cannot be separated easily, or for long; they are both within us each day and each night. Neither need be feared or avoided.

I need not avoid thinking about death or keep it separate it from life. I can allow it to be incorporated into my understanding of life.

Understanding Friends

"When my mom died, many of the friends who helped us were people we met who had also recently had loved ones die. They knew how to support me; they weren't afraid of saying the wrong thing. They also knew the importance of being there. I was thankful to be surrounded by people who could openly show support during the dark times, yet also embrace the beauty of living."

Monica Nelson, in loving memory of her mother, Creta Mullenmaster.

In addition to our relatives and the friends we already have, we may meet new people who can help us affirm our grief. Those who have had losses in their own lives may be especially supportive; it's often easy to become friends, since they understand to a large degree what we are going through. They may be particularly helpful by doing those things that others may be reluctant to do, such as sending a card on our loved one's birthday, or on the anniversary of their death. They also may be more likely to say our loved one's name.

These friends help us to be ourselves during difficult times. They are to be cherished, for they are likely to stay with us even during our worst moments.

I am thankful for the friends who really understand and support me. Today I will talk or write to one of them, telling them how much they mean to me.

The Power of Touch

"Strength and love can come through gentle, soothing touch."

    Anonymous

We are caught up in a world that depends largely on language to convey our feelings and thoughts. Yet there are many times when words seem inadequate or even meaningless. This is especially true in grief. A hand upon our own, a warm embrace, a tender kiss, all tell us that we are cared for and that others share our pain. More than words, these actions communicate strength, understanding, and love.

When words seem inadequate, I will seek the gentle touch of those family members and friends that are my support. I can receive consolation and love from others.

Pressure to Return to "Normal"

"My family is so worried about me. They want the 'old' Dianne back again. What they don't know is that they will never get her back. I've changed!"

Dianne Ostby, in loving memory of her miscarried babies, and Lauren Brianne, her infant daughter who lived for seventeen days.

Our family, relatives, and co-workers want so much to see us recovered, healed, and whole again. They may mistakenly feel that they can and should help us find that "old, normal self" who seems to be temporarily lost. They may see this as their role. They may also be seeking security for themselves; they *knew* who we were before, and how to act around us. This new person is unknown to them.

We have changed. We cannot go back and be the person we once were. We are developing into a new state of 'normal.' Others may be slow to recognize this, but with our help and honesty, in time they will likely respect the new and changed person we are. Still, we may need to ask them not to pressure us to try to go backwards. Even though we may want to do this ourselves, it really is not possible. Each event and new day changes us.

I am changed. I cannot go backwards. I can work towards accepting my new sense of normalcy and ask others to respect me for who I am today.

Feeling Helpless

"It is a very helpless feeling to not be able to rescue or save your child. Death is a very cold, hard fact of life to accept."

> *Dawn Fern, in memory of her children, Nichol Michele and Aaron Michael, and her grandmother, Maude V. Dull.*

No matter the age of our loved one or their relationship to us, we may feel partially responsible for their death and wish we could have saved them. Our lack of control may leave us feeling helpless. We may think we let them down, and be overly hard on ourselves.

It may help for us to repeat to ourselves that we do not have control over life and death—that power rests somewhere else. We loved them and still love them, and we can trust that they knew this.

I can acknowledge the feelings of helplessness I have. When I have these feelings, I will remember that I have no control over life and death. I will stop blaming myself.

Remembering Our Loved One's
Sense of Humor

"Some time before she died, my mom turned to me and said, 'When I die, I want you to have a Manhattan and a cigarette on me. And why don't you do something about my double chins!' How I cherish my mom's terrific sense of humor."

Julie Faxvog, in loving memory of her mom, Charlotte Margaret Joan Doherty Klug.

Laughter and humor may still not hold a high priority for us. Yet the memory of our loved one's own sense of humor or their appreciation of a good joke can help us cope with their death. Julie's Mom had a reputation for being a tease, and her antics were a delight to her family. These memories brighten Julie's days and give her strength.

Recalling the laughter, the lighter side of life, may help us through the difficult times that continue to be a part of our lives. The relief that a sense of humor brings can make us feel just a bit better. It can allow our damaged spirit to dance, if even for a short time.

There is humor all about me, if I just let it in. By remembering my loved one's sense of humor, I can find a place for it in my life and let it help soothe my grief.

Covering Up Feelings In Public

"People said I was 'so strong' and 'so brave.' I may have looked that way on the outside, but that's not at all how I felt on the inside. I was good at covering up in public."
 Norma Long Wood

How adept we can become at putting up a false front and acting as if everything is okay! Yet behind our facade lies our very real, very private pain.

Often we are reluctant to grieve in front of others because we don't want to be vulnerable. We fear that we will be rejected, shamed, or labelled as weak. This is not to say we have to be vulnerable with everyone, nor do we have to feel guilty about this. Still, we may want to find one or more people with whom we feel safe enough to share our grief. If we have some support we may not feel so alone.

I have a right to grieve in my own way, to share my pain with those I choose. I don't have to act strong for others.

Fear of Additional Tragedy

"We were afraid that more tragedy would befall us, that God would take our son Matthew to punish us further. We became afraid that somehow evil had come to live in our house. We were afraid of the dark, literally. We slept with a nightlight on for over a year."

> Steve and Mary Van Bockern; "We miss you, Catie."

Losing a loved one is a terrible experience. In trying to cope with our loss, we may feel that we have been singled out for disaster, and worry that our future will be filled with one unfortunate event after the other. Suddenly, we feel vulnerable and mortal. Like Steve and Mary, fear may begin to permeate our days and nights.

More than anything, we may want some assurance that we will not suffer further harm. We want to feel protected and insulated from additional tragedy. We have sacrificed enough.

Trying to control everything around us—from the darkness to what roads we choose to drive on—is common. For now, this may be how we attempt to find peace in what feels like a chaotic and frightening world.

If I am concerned about further tragedy, I will focus on those things that help me feel safe and secure. I can seek peace.

The Difficult Times of the Day and Week

"I'm glad I had work to return to, but the nights and weekends were terribly lonely. I just wanted to hibernate or run away, push away the pain."

Cathy Copenhaver, in memory of her father, Henry W. Dock.

Being distracted with work and other activities keeps our minds busy, so we tend to think about our loved one's death a little less. But we all experience times of the day which are hard for us. Some of us may find it difficult to get up in the morning, or we may notice our loved one's absence more during the "down" times like evenings, weekends, or during dinner. We may feel particularly lonely or empty at these times.

We may try to avoid these tough times by making our lives even busier. Yet, as active as we keep ourselves, the emptiness cannot be completely filled or avoided forever. We may find it helpful to allow these times to come, and deal with them as they arise. Reading, meditating, praying, writing, or seeking out a peaceful place are a few things which might prove helpful during these times.

I will deal with the hard times of the day or week as they come, and find ways to get through these times without filling my every minute.

Deciding Not to Worry About Tomorrow

"Don't borrow on tomorrow's sorrows."
   Anonymous

With our loved one gone, the future may intimidate or frighten us. The uncertainty of tomorrow and the days ahead can be stressful. We may worry that other bad things will happen, and we might try to protect ourselves from further pain. Many of us have trouble imagining that we will ever be able to love someone this much again. We may be afraid of the pain and sorrow that will follow if we suffer another loss.

Instead of borrowing on tomorrow's sorrow, we may need to give our all to living for today. We may suffer again someday, but that cannot be controlled. To really live is to love again, trust again, and invest in our happiness. If we do not risk, we stay where we are, feeling our pain over and over again.

I can face today and tomorrow with hope, and not worry about tomorrow. I am willing to risk future pain in order to live my life to the fullest.

Multiple Losses

"Both my parents died within the same year. The initial experience of grief, pain, loss and the terrible, empty silence was overwhelming. The inability to integrate and experience these feelings before my second parent died was for me the entering point of the center of human pain."

Dr. Beverly Musgrave, in loving memory of her parents, Mr. & Mrs. Fred P. Musgrave.

Sadly, Beverly is not alone. Many of us must grieve the loss of more than one family member or friend in a short period of time. Coping with these multiple deaths is horrendously difficult. Our suffering feels endless, and it may feel as if we're taking ten steps backward for every half step forward. Sorting through our jumbled feelings is almost impossible. We may feel depressed and tormented. We want the pain to end; we want the tragedies to stop.

Coping with multiple catastrophes can be over-whelming. It is important that we depend on the support of valued and understanding friends, take good physical care of ourselves, and not place unrealistic expectations on ourselves.

I know there are no easy answers, so I will take one day at a time as I cope and survive. I can look for one small bright spot in my day.

Rationalizations Of Our
Loved One's Death

"One important thing that has helped us deal with our sister's premature death is the knowledge that she died quickly. The doctor stated that it was his feeling that no matter how much he tried to resuscitate her, she would not have come back. This was comforting to our whole family."

Pastor Mike Zylstra, in loving memory of his sister Mary, who died in a car accident.

Each of us may find ourselves seeking peace at different times by recalling things in our loved one's life or death that somehow let us rationalize what has happened. Perhaps we find comfort in the knowledge that they didn't suffer, or that no matter what interventions might have been tried, our loved one could not have been saved. Or, we might think about the pain they had been going through and feel thankful that they are at rest.

Although we do not need to search for justifications for our loved one's death, we may find comfort in these consoling thoughts, at least on those days when we feel the need.

If I need to, I can seek consolation and comfort in rationalizations of my loved one's death.

Our Loved One's Contributions to Our Life

"Each individual is endowed with certain instruments and we hear the music of their lives long after they are gone... The music that was set in motion by my daughter's love, hope, and faith will move, everlasting, in sweet memories forever."

Bill Boggs, TCF, in loving memory of his daughter, Anne, who was kidnapped and murdered.

The presence of our loved one enriched our own life. This loss saddens us. Still, their unique contributions—the splendid music they created—continues to fill our life as we preserve their dreams, hopes, and love. Though they have gone, all our loved one gave and promised to give is held forever in our hearts.

I am grateful for the presence of my loved one in my life. I will tenderly remember the splendid music they created just for me.

Needing to Feel Close

"Sometimes I get the box with Jesse's things in it and I can still smell him on his little sleeper and I feel closer to him. I worry if it's crazy to do this. I don't want to go crazy."
Susan Price, in memory of her son, Jesse Lee.

Our need to feel close to our loved one is quite natural. There is nothing crazy about wanting to remember or feel near. We miss our loved one. We want to keep their memory fresh in our hearts and minds.

Whether we gently finger each item in our keepsake box or slip off into sleep to dream of long ago moments, there may always be a special item, place, or time that holds the memory of our loved one more tightly. These things help secure the past and never let our loved one drift too far away.

It is not crazy to want to remember and feel close to my loved one. I will find ways to seek closeness to them, keeping my memories fresh in my heart and mind.

Feeling Shunned

"Those whose worlds are still intact cannot understand
The agony of being denied future memories.
I have become a social leper.
To many who look upon my pain,
I bring deep fear that it is contagious.
They back away and disappear."

        Lynnette Kay Titus, in loving memory of her son,
Ryan.

It is distressing when others avoid and shun us. No one wants to be a social leper. Those who shy away from us may do so because they don't know how to help us. They may fear that asking about our loved one will just upset us or bring up painful memories. They may think it's easier to be absent or silent then to risk injuring us more.

Most people are not hurtful on purpose. Knowing how to help a bereaved person often takes having been deeply touched by pain. Without this experience, people simply may not know how best to reach out. We must try not to be bitter or resentful.

I am responsible for my own feelings. I can be disappointed if people avoid or shun me, but I will try not to take offense where none is intended.

Reflections and Thankfulness

"Reflecting can be a very sad, even disturbing pastime. But one can hardly expect to live on a continuous high. The sad times can be defended if we are wise enough to be thankful that our lives were, and still are, touched by people we feel to be so special."

Edna Miner Larson, in loving memory of her mother, late husband, and her friend, Trudy.

Reflecting on our loved ones and our own changing lives can bring intense moments. While tears and sorrowful thoughts may come, it usually doesn't take long to find the special people, relationships, and blessings that currently are ours. When we remember our blessings, we can better embrace the beauty brought to us through our loved ones' lives. For this we can find thankfulness.

I can spend time reflecting on my loved one, my life, and my past. As I move towards my future, I can recall at least two reasons why I am thankful.

Learning to Accept Support

"Nothing is impossible to a willing heart."
John Heywood

Oftentimes our loved one's death leaves us feeling discouraged about life. Going on without them is a struggle. If we're willing, though, life *can* get better.

An important step in this direction is to accept support from others, even though we may not be used to it. The companionship and understanding that others can offer may help combat our feelings of loneliness and give us hope that with their help, we can survive.

Coping with the changes brought about by our loved one's death is not easy. By accepting the support of others, we may find our grief a little easier to bear.

I am willing to let others in my life. I will accept their understanding and support.

Pressures of Daily Living

"I still have my moments—burned applesauce, wool socks that shrink, and missed appointments."

Tree Johnson, in loving memory of her husband, Bruce, who was killed in a car accident.

With the passing of some time, we often think we *should* be much better, and we put pressure on ourselves to be *all well*. Yet ordinary tasks and decision-making may still be challenging at times. We may find ourselves missing meetings or classes, losing things, burning dinner, or noticing too late that our car is out of gas.

This is grief and sorrow. Our minds and spirits are still remembering and hurting. We are distracted. It is natural to still find simple tasks overwhelming or to suffer memory lapses, even months after our loved one's death.

I will not pressure myself to be in control of all of my daily activities. I will allow myself to forget and make mistakes, accepting this as normal. I will not judge myself harshly.

Letting Grief Take its Course

"Don't hurry the pain. Each day it will ebb or flow, and it always will to a certain extent. There will always be a smell or place or something that will reopen the wound, but each time it gets a little easier to move along. It builds a certain tender strength."

Sonja Fowler, in memory of Baby Fowler.

At times we may want to hurry and be done with our grieving. We want the hurt and sorrow to finally stop. Yet, as Sonja experienced, our grief must take its own course, ebbing and flowing at will. Much as we would like, we cannot control or force the pace of our grieving.

Still, as we heal we may find that our grief lessens and becomes easier to manage at times. We have gained strength and, without realizing it, our grief has changed all on its own. Grief has taken its own course.

I will not be in a hurry to grieve the loss of my loved one. I can let grief move at its own pace. I will build strength as it ebbs and flows.

Loneliness

"My rage has subsided...loneliness has set in. A longing to see him, be with him, call him."

    Michelle Dubreuil, in loving memory of her brother, Rich.

Michelle has moved from feeling intense rage over her brother's death to experiencing the aching sting of loneliness. Our loneliness is often born out of isolation and feelings of abandonment. By now, those who stood by us in the early days of our loved's one death have likely returned to their own lives. Other family and friends may have also left, so that they might heal their own hurts or return to a normal routine. For now, we may feel alone with our grief and our loneliness.

We miss our loved one. We wish desperately to share just one more "I love you," one more goodbye. Life may feel empty, and we may believe that we have been abandoned not only by our loved one, but also by our friends and family.

Just as rage gave way to loneliness, so too loneliness will give way to yet another set of feelings. For now, we can look for the strength that is in our heart and seek out those among us who can lend us support, compassion, and understanding.

The absence of my loved one leaves me aching for them. I miss them, and life feels empty without them. I will break out of my loneliness today by finding a supportive friend to share some time with me.

Facing The Future

"The sound of her silk skirt has stopped.
On the marble pavement dust grows.
Her empty room is cold and still.
Fallen leaves are piled against the doors.
  Longing for that lovely lady...
How can I bring my aching heart to rest?"

  from ***Chinese Poems***, *by Han Wu-ti, translated*
by Arthur Waley.

To go on in life without our loved one can be heartwrenching. Many of us can still scarcely imagine a future in which our loved one does not play a major role. We may still be filled with uncertainty and doubt, and have little confidence we will be able to live a fulfilling life.

We can, however, learn to rebuild our lives and find happiness again. We can reinvest in family and friends, activities, school, or work. We might take a new job, try a new hobby, or seek out new or lapsed friendships.

The responsibility for planning our future and living our lives rests in our hands. The choice is ours: we can face the future alone and afraid, or choose to believe that life is worth living again and work to develop a future filled with promise and hope.

My heart aches when I think about facing the future without my loved one. Still, I know that I can take personal responsibility for my future. I have choices. I will seriously consider my options as I reengage in life.

Meeting Ourself in Our Sorrow

"A quote translated from Dante has fixed in my mind since reading it: 'In the middle of the journey of our life I came to myself in a dark wood.' Few emotions offer better opportunity to meet oneself than sorrow."

Colleen Kent, in memory of the contributions her family and friends have made to her life.

For many of us, our loved one's death has brought us to the 'dark woods' of our life. The encounter may be an invitation to find ourselves. Here we may confront our ultimate fears, and possibly resolve our feelings about death and life, love and hate. Making our way through the 'dark woods' will be a lonely and difficult task. We must draw upon the courage and strength which is within ourselves.

My loved one's death has brought me to the 'dark woods.' I will have the courage and strength to find myself.

Saying Our Loved One's Name

"After my husband died, I remember how people used to change the subject whenever his name came up. They didn't want to upset me. But not talking was more upsetting. I remember yelling at someone once, 'He really did exist, he really was a part of my life. Don't treat me like he was never even alive!'"

> *Annette Malinsky, in loving memory of her husband, Dr. Howard Malinsky.*

After someone dies, the clock continues to tick, the world still turns, and after awhile, most of our support people go on about their business. Then one day we may realize that no one has said our loved one's name out loud for a long time, and friends and relatives may have even avoided mentioning our loved one except in vague terms.

This silence can become even louder and more painful over time. We may wonder whether relatives and friends have really forgotten this special person, whether they are so uncomfortable that they don't dare try to talk about them. Or, maybe they are worried that by reminding us of our loved one we will be hurt again.

Whatever the reason, if others don't use our loved one's name, we can be the one to break the ice and say it out loud; we can guide them to what will be helpful to us. If we take the lead, others may become more willing to take a risk and do the same. Our actions may encourage others.

If I want to hear my loved one's name but others are avoiding it, I can work to change things. I can say their name in the presence of others and help all of us to become more comfortable over time.

Allowing Ourselves to Laugh Again

"I laugh and enjoy myself. It's not the same, of course, but life is still fun and well worth living. This new chapter of my life is good, but it is punctuated with moments of sadness. Life goes on. So do we."

> *Patrick Page, in loving memory of his wife, Marjorie.*

There may be many times when we feel we shouldn't laugh or be happy again. It can almost seem as if we are being disloyal to our loved one. Yet we can only stay serious and intense for so long. Our spirits need a chance to dance and soar. Our loved one would want this for us. In order for us to truly honor them and grieve for them, we will need the lighter moments to balance the painful times.

In my loss and sorrow I can seek interludes of joy and humor. These moments will help provide balance to the heavy work of mourning.

Being Alone Brings Changes

"Except when company came, I could never sit alone at the table to eat a meal after my husband died. It was just too hard and lonely."

Genevieve Kriesch, in memory of her beloved husband, Norman.

With the death of our loved one came many changes in our lives; we may now be experiencing a startling sense of isolation. It may be hard to endure things that we took for granted before; walking down the aisles of the grocery store, going to church or to the synagogue, watching television, attending baby showers or weddings, or just getting up in the morning. Our habits and routines have been altered. This has become a time of new beginnings.

It may be a long time, if ever, before we are able to go back to those same daily routines. We have conflicting needs. We struggle with the reality of our loved one's absence, unable or unwilling to let things be the same now that they are gone. Yet with our very being we want our loved one back, so we can return to the routines which were once ours.

In my loneliness and sorrow, I can allow my routine and habits to change along with my new reality. These changes are helpful to me as I grieve and move forward to new beginnings.

Seeking Answers

"There are things that are known and things that are unknown: in between are doors."
   Anonymous

There is so much of our loved one's death that is unknown to us. We have a hundred whys, but few answers. At times we may feel confused, frustrated, and disturbed. We want to make sense of our tragedy.

We do not know what lies between the known and unknown. It may be truth or illusion. Yet we can open the doors that are available to us and find the answers that are there.

If I still have many unanswered questions about my loved one's death, I can look for the answers that are available to me.

Keeping Perspective While
Regaining Some Control

"I've given up trying to control the outside world, my feelings, and my mood swings. I realize there is little I **can** *control, except on certain days when I can decide how I will respond to things."*
Anonymous

While there may have been a time when we believed we had control over much of our lives, our loved one's death may have destroyed this belief. Over the past months, our emotional journey has continually reminded us how little we *do* control. Eventually, however, we may gain some balance as we work towards a more realistic sense of control.

To regain trust and a little control in our lives, we may have to start small. Maybe we can control how angry we get when someone says something hurtful, or maybe we can make choices about more routine things that don't involve intense emotions. When we have a healthy respect for our need to control, we will likely feel better about ourselves—less like a victim, and yet not invincible either.

I will remind myself that I am not all powerful, nor do I need to be a victim with no control. Today I will take control of one small piece of my life.

Wanting Our Loved One Back

"I knew that no place in our Bible are we promised our children will outlive us; yet my heart ached so to have my son back."

> *Nina S. Nesbit, in memory of her son, Stanley Wayne.*

Like Nina, many of us expect that our children will outlive us. As parents, we see ourselves giving and nurturing life, not being witness to our child's death. We may feel our role as parent was to keep them safe. Having to go on without them may see like a horrible, cruel trick.

Most of us never really expect or feel prepared for the death of our loved one. Whether we lose our child, partner, parent, sibling, or close friend, we are devastated. Our loved one should be with us. This is not how life should be. Death has stolen the one we love, and we want them back.

My loved one's death has been devastating. This is not how I thought life would be. My heart aches for my loved one.

We Remember Them

from **Gates of Prayer**, *Reform Judaism Prayerbook*

In the rising of the sun and in its going down,
We remember them;

In the blowing of the wind and in the chill of winter,
We remember them;

In the opening of buds and in the warmth of summer,
We remember them;

In the rustling of leaves and the beauty of autumn,
We remember them;

In the beginning of the year and when it ends,
We remember them;

When we are weary and in need of strength,
We remember them;

When we are lost and sick at heart,
We remember them;

When we have joys we yearn to share,
We remember them;

So long as we live, they too shall live,
for they are now a part of us as

We remember them.

The Uneven Path

Trusting in God

"So lean on Him and even though
Today the sky's not blue,
Trust in His great, unending love
And know He cares for you."
        Annette Lassahn

For many, the deep sense of grief and sorrow we feel rekindles our need for God. Having been taught as children that we could lean on God during times of trouble or suffering, we may now look to Him for consolation. We rely on His understanding and deep care and we draw encouragement knowing that He is walking alongside us.

I can lean on God and others and be supported by them. I can find comfort when I need to.

Strength and Staying Behind

"I'm glad that I'm the one who was left to go through this. I'm strong and I can make it. I wouldn't have wanted her to have to handle this sorrow and pain, facing the world and the future without her partner. It's better that she died first, rather than me. This is pain that she has been able to avoid."

Keith Parks, in loving memory of his first wife, Darlene.

There are times when we may find solace in being the one who stayed behind. Though we are lonely and hurting, we don't wish this pain on our loved one. We may find some comfort knowing they are at peace, even though we struggle. While this thought will not be at the forefront of our minds every day, it may help soothe us during the rocky times.

When I need consolation, I can turn to the comforting thought that my loved one was not left behind.

Memories Obscured By Pain

"Memories are fragile. They can be lost. Far better to bear the pain of them, which will pass, and hold fast to every image."

> Marie-Claire Davis, in memory of her beloved George.

Memories of our loved one are very precious images, yet sometimes their beauty is obscured by our pain. There are times when it may be difficult to see healthy or happy pictures of our loved one or recall special occasions, like birthdays, anniversaries, or holidays. These images may trigger feelings of loneliness and remind us how much we miss them. Still, each memory is priceless. Eventually the pain will lessen and each memory may grow more wonderful with time.

The memories of my loved one are precious to me. Though they may be obscured by pain at times, I will hold fast to each and every one.

Getting Back on Track

"'Hold 'em in the row.' When my mother was a child she used to pick cotton in a field. An old mule would pull a cart through the field to collect the full bags of cotton. There were deep ruts in which the wagon would travel between the rows of cotton. Periodically, that old mule would wander off to one side or the other and pull that wagon out of the ruts. It took a number of people to get the mule and cart back on a straight course.

"My mother always used this story to help me look at my problems. She would offer various suggestions and always end with, 'Hold 'em in the row.'"

Ken Pugh, in loving memory of his mother.

The death of our loved one may have forced us off our safe and familiar path. To "hold 'em in the row," we may need to ask our family and friends for their support and understanding, today and in the coming days. We often need help to face our pain, to believe and trust that we can and will survive.

My life has gotten off track. I can ask others to help me as I work to get my life in order and become determined to survive.

Seeking Out Kindred Spirits

"My healing began when I came in touch with other suicide survivors."

   Mary Swanson, in loving memory of her son, Brad, who was a victim of suicide.

Healing begins at different places for each of us. Many of us find that talking and being with others who have had a similar experience is affirming and helpful. It can be difficult to try to tell someone how we feel, the enormity of our pain, and what we need, particularly if they haven't been there themselves. If we do find someone who knows this kind of pain, we may feel like kindred spirits, or two people in a foreign land who speak the same language.

If I feel that it will be helpful, I will seek out others who have had a similar experience. I can be affirmed by their understanding and support.

Lost Hopes and Expectations

"Nathan was supposed to hang on long enough for them to find a cure, finally become a healthy kid and start catching up with all his friends who had passed him by, just like when he beat the leukemia. Instead, he curled up for a nap while he waited for his mom to bring him a special dinner, and he slipped away."

Dan J. Henderson, in loving memory of his son, Nathan.

How many endless hours we spent waiting, wondering, and praying. We may have waited for a cure, prayed for a miracle, and expected a full recovery. Yet despite all our efforts, our loved one still died, and their death cruelly robbed us of our hopes and dreams. How we wish we could change the past. How we wish we could have made our loved one's life better. All our expectations have shattered; our dreams have disappeared. Letting go of our loved one and our hopes and plans is not how we wanted life to be.

I had so many hopes and expectations for my loved one and our life together. I'm sad that they're all lost. I will begin to develop some new expectations as I slowly heal.

Our Loved Ones Become a Part of Us

"What we have once enjoyed deeply we can never lose. All that we love deeply becomes a part of us."
  Helen Keller

Those we love never really leave us, even in death. Their face, their smile, their scent may fade over time, yet the essence of who they are is the legacy we carry into the future. They have become a part of us, our past, our beliefs. Our picture of the world includes their influence. They are now a part of us.

On both good days and difficult days I will remember that my loved one is with me. We are joined and intertwined forever.

Surrounded by Tears and Silence

"Still I yearn to see his eyes looking at me and to hear his cry in the night. But for now, I am surrounded by silence and blinded by my own tears."

Patrice Thomas, in memory of Matthew Anthony, her beloved son.

Though we may be surrounded with people and have other things to live for in our lives, there are times when we ache and yearn for our loved one's touch, sounds, and presence. Sadly, they are gone, and we are starkly aware of the silence that engulfs us. In spite of all we have to be thankful for, this silence can become overwhelming. Still, it is a connection to them.

Through tears of love and sorrow I can experience the silence as a reminder of one I hold dear.

Finding Peace When Visiting the Grave

"This is the first time I visited the grave and did not cry. So much healing has taken place, but much more must come."

Suzanne Knopf, in loving memory of her son, Jamieson Sean.

Visiting the grave or special place of our loved one can be painful, especially when our grief is fresh, and on special occasions. Still, there will likely come a time when we notice that healing has taken place; maybe we are not as pained during our visits, or perhaps we feel a sense of peace. This doesn't mean we will never feel sorrow or sadness for our loved one again, but it does mean that we are changing and moving through our grief. Peace, joy, relief, and acceptance may come and go. We must allow ourselves to receive these gifts of healing.

I can accept that my feelings will change as I move through my grief. When I am sad I will let that be, and I will leave room for the joy and peace.

Accepting Challenge

"Life can only be understood backwards; but it must be lived forwards."
*from **Life**, by Sören Kierkegaard.*

It is a challenge to face our grief. We may argue that we cannot possibly meet this challenge, or say that we are just not ready. The very nature of the word "challenge," however, is to be daring; to dare to grow, change, and succeed. To move beyond the pain, to survive, we must accept the challenge—the dare—that our loved one's death has presented to us.

I can see the challenge that the loss of my loved one has created. I acknowledge this challenge. I will face a small portion of my grief today.

Broken Dreams

"Ross was always here when I needed him. Then a cruel twist of fate cancelled all our dreams. My Ross died."
　　　Dru Weyls, in memory of her beloved husband, Ross.

When our loved one dies, we may feel that we have been let down. There were plans we shared, dreams we dreamt, and the promise of a future together, if only in our hearts. We believed we would be together for much longer. We did not expect to have to say goodbye, plan their funeral, or live without them. We needed them and had plans and hopes that included them, even if we had some warning or knew in our heads, if not in our hearts, that they would die someday.

It is natural to feel let down, to be distressed by the unfulfilled and broken dreams. We want to make them whole and beautiful again. But for now, they are just painful reminders. In time, the beauty and wholeness will return, though some pain will always remain.

In the broken dreams and promises I can remember my loved one's specialness.

More Good Days Than Bad

"About six or seven months after my son died, I noticed that lately I had been having many more good days than bad. I still thought about Brennan every day, but it wasn't always as painful. I felt hopeful that I could survive and be happy again someday."

Sherokee Ilse, in memory of her son, Brennan William.

At some point, each of us may notice that we are experiencing more good days than bad. For some, this may come a few months after our loved one's death; for others, it may take many months; and for some of us, it may take even longer to feel hopeful and have happy thoughts again.

We may need to help ourselves move in this direction by continuing to find outlets for our feelings and ways to share our loss and memories. We may also need to do nice things for ourselves; see a movie, wear bright colors, watch a sunset, buy something special, bring home flowers, or begin planning something that we can look forward to.

I will seek more good days to balance the hard ones. Today I will do something special to help me feel better.

The Courage to Face Our Fears

"We cannot conquer fear. We can only hope to acknowledge it, respect it and live with it. We think of those who stand in the face of fear as being courageous. Yet, we all have courage. We are all courageous."
     Darcie Sims, in loving memory of her son, Austin.

Many of us are so anxious about our fears that we have trouble even acknowledging them. We may have looked at others and said, "How did they survive a crisis like that? They are so brave and courageous. I could never do that." We may think that we don't have the courage to survive a tragedy like theirs. We might be afraid for them, and for ourselves.

Yet we are living through a major trauma. If we look inside ourselves we might realize that we *can* handle our pain and fears; we *are* courageous. It is amazing to see what we are capable of handling. Though we may have been worried, we are surviving.

I am courageous. I am surviving, and I can face my fears and continue to survive.

Finding Peace and Solitude in Nature

"When I see a sunset, spring rain, beautiful billowing clouds, the colors and smell of fall in the air, I can't help but feel the goodness of nature and the closeness of my loved ones."

    Monica Nelson, in loving memory of her mother, Creta Mullenmaster.

A moonlit night, a spring flower, a quiet backyard: the beauty of nature can bring us peace and solitude as we experience life's mysteries. Through new eyes we may be able to enjoy the miracle of nature and life. Many of us may find a special closeness to our loved ones who have died as we sit watching a sunset or a peaceful lake or river. While we may be especially aware of our aloneness at these times, this may also be a quiet time of reflection, inspiration, and connectedness with those we love.

I will take time to smell the flowers, watch a sunset, and experience the beauty of nature as I remember those I love.

Love and Regrets

"I loved them and still love them. There are so many things I wish I could have told them. I just trust that they know."

> *Cara Duffey, in memory of her twins, Kara and Kayla.*

After a loved one dies it is natural to want to feel reassured that they knew we loved them. We may have regrets about unfinished business or important messages left unspoken.

If we hadn't said those special words, "I love you," recently, we may wonder if they really knew how we felt. Perhaps we had a disagreement or there were ill feelings prior to their death, or maybe words of affection simply were hard for us to say. Or, we might have been far away from them and not had the opportunity to say goodbye and share our special messages of love.

Nearly all of us have some concerns or regrets about things we didn't say before our loved one died. Hopefully we can take comfort by looking back on their life, even if it was short, and remember the good times; those messages of love we did share are our togetherness.

Even though I may have regrets, I can remember the ways I did show my love and appreciation. I can trust that they knew my feelings. I can also tell them how much I love them by sharing special thoughts even now, through writing, prayer, or letting my soul speak to them.

Living in the Present

*"If we fill our days with regrets over yesterdays,
and with worries for the tomorrows,
we will have no today in which to be thankful."*
Anonymous

Living in the present is not easy, even many months after our loved one has died. We may find ourselves reliving their last days, thinking of the things we could have done differently. It may be hard to let go of the blame, shame, or guilt that we may still feel. Or, we may spend a great deal of energy planning, worrying, and trying to control our future. All of this keeps us from living today.

Today is all we have. Yesterday is gone and can't be changed. And who knows what tomorrow will bring? The moment for living is now; we may need to remind ourselves of that. We can make the most of this day, finding reasons to feel thankful and making this day special to us and to others.

I can focus on the joys of today and the special people who still surround me.

Looking for a Saving Grace
in Our Suffering

"Lord, somehow I don't understand. Please help me. I am so afraid, so lost and confused. God, if you are so loving and caring, why do we have to sit here and suffer? Lord, I know that we all go through trials. But losing my brother wasn't on my list."

Heidi Stallings, in loving memory of her brother, David, whose life and memory she holds close to her heart.

It may be hard to comprehend why God allows us to suffer. If He is a benevolent God, then why does He allow us to experience such wrenching pain? We know that the hurt we feel is not hidden from Him. What, then, can be the reason for our suffering?

While it may be impossible for us to pinpoint a reason, at some point we may unexpectedly find some small shred of good coming from our devastating loss. To our surprise, we may find the delicate petals of a flower pushing out from the ashes of our grief.

For now, the reason for my suffering is not important. I will think awhile about the new possibilities life has presented to me.

The Messages of Our Loved Ones

"My friend Julie's answering machine says, 'You have thirty seconds to leave your message.' I leave the answer, 'No, I have the rest of my life.' It is a joke—and yet it isn't. All of those whose loss I have felt have left their messages. In loss I can still recount them, and in quiet space I may find other answers."

Colleen Kent, in loving memory to those she called friend. (Colleen Kent died in a car accident a few weeks after writing these lines, never knowing how little time she really had.)

Yes, our loved ones have left their messages; some helpful, encouraging, or supportive, some damaging and destructive. We find these messages in the things they created, both in their relationships and handiwork, in the things they felt passionately about, and in the words they attempted to live by. These messages are woven tightly into our lives, often in unexpected ways.

The mark our loved one left on our life may have vastly enriched us. Or, if the messages were hurtful, we may feel distressed and injured. Colleen tells us that we "may find other answers." If we feel harmed by our loved one, we can try to draw new conclusions from the messages left us and seek understanding from the answers which may come.

My life is filled with messages from my loved one. I can reflect on these messages so that they better encourage and support me.

Growing Stronger

"There are days when I feel my life has changed. I have grown stronger in mind, body, and soul. I am now ready to let go of some of the pain and go on to the next step."
          Suzanne Knopf, in loving memory of her son, Jamieson Sean.

As a result of the long struggle to survive and live again, our endurance and resilience develops. The ups and downs of the journey test us, causing us to find support and inner strength. There may be times when we realize that in spite of the adversity, we have grown stronger. This can be one of the positives that grows out of our loss.

I have survived through difficult times, and my spirit and strength have grown. I can appreciate these changes as I let go of some of the pain and heartache.

Life Is Looking Up

"Surprisingly, life is looking up. I never thought that I would see this day. Sadness, the melancholy moments, the longing to have him back, they will always be with me. But now I see a shimmering light in the distance. I am pulling my life together, making right choices, consulting my brother as I go along and knowing he's watching over us."

Michelle Dubreuil, in memory of her friend and brother, Rich.

What a surprise it is when our life begins to look better! Our grief has been a rollercoaster of feelings, few of them pleasant. The thought of having fun, smiling again, or even having a good bellylaugh were unthinkable. Yet the day does come when we feel a bit better, as if the worst has passed. Strength and calmness replace sorrow and depression. We know our grief has not gone away; it is just less intense and less frequent. We can find light off in the distance. Though we may never be totally over the death of our loved one, we can get through it.

I can see my life looking up. My good days outweigh the bad. I enjoy life more each day.

Drawing Creativity Out of Pain

"Although I had painted off and on for years, six months after my husband died I started classes again. That whole year, it seems, I spent time in my basement surrounded by brightly colored paintings of flowers."

Maggie Merkow, in memory of her loving husband, Rob.

Out of darkness and despair there seems to be a natural need to express ourselves and work our way towards light and healing. Creating something out of our pain can usually make us feel better and can be a visible tribute to our loved one, a way to give life or give *to* life. Writing poetry or prose, keeping a journal, painting, enjoying music, woodcrafting, or drawing are but a few of the many ways we can express our inner feelings. Our personal creations can come from our pain and love.

I can make something out of my feelings of despair by finding a creative way to express myself.

Recapturing Our Loved One's Spirit

"Sometimes I wander away to a place where no one can go but me, and I live with Kenneth for awhile."
Josie Khan Comphel, in memory of Kenneth.

There are times when we long to be with our loved one's spirit. At these moments, we may escape from the everyday world and let our minds and souls join them. The intimacy and closeness we feel may bring us tears and joy as we sit with our thoughts and remember all that we can about them.

I can be close and seek an intimate connectedness with my loved one's spirit when I need to.

Choosing Life and Hope

"At least now there are days when I realize that nothing I can do will bring my father back. I can choose to either continue being sad and mourn what I have lost, or live my own life while appreciating his memories. I'm ready to move on, cherishing those gifts."

Barbara Ilse, in loving memory of her father, Wesley Booman.

It is natural to lament and become immersed in self-pity when a special person we love has died. This is an important part of the grieving process. Still, we can only feel sad and upset for so long. Being overly consumed by sadness for too long can lead to illness and a sense of hopelessness. This is one choice.

Another choice is to seek to recapture the joy and beauty that our loved one's life brought us. We can consider how we have changed because of them and remember the gifts we received from them. It's up to us to determine how we will keep their memory alive, in our heart and within our family.

We can decide between life and hope or long-term sadness and despair. No one can make that choice for us.

When I am ready, I will carefully consider my choices for living and moving on. I will take time to consider the gifts and precious memories that I have received through my loved one's life.

A Place for Finding Peace

"When we go to the pine grove where Bruce and Jonas' bodies lie in the beautiful earth in the coffins we made by hand, I burn candles and cedar and sing circle songs. How can I not be uplifted and feel loved by God?"

Tree Johnson, in loving memory of her son, Jonas, and husband, Bruce.

Having a special spot to go to remember our loved one may help us to seek peace and solitude at times. If we don't have such a place, or can't go there physically, we can let our minds wander to one that brings us calm feelings.

What we do in this special place will be unique and right for us. We may pray, meditate, bring gifts, sing, or do whatever moves our hearts to recapture our loved one's spirit and find calmness.

When I need uplifting and closeness with my loved one, I can journey to a special place. I can seek solitude and peace with my God or higher power.

Feeling Tenderhearted

"I feel so tenderhearted since David's death. It's like being one of the walking wounded. Hearing about a child getting hurt, an accident, or other tragedy makes my heart bleed. I cry for them, but I also cry for me."

Charlene Nelson, in loving memory of her dear son, David.

Having once experienced the anguish and devastation of death, many of us are quick to feel compassion for others. We may now have a keener, more acute sense of sympathy. Yet, many times we may be stunned and unprepared for the intensity of our reactions. When our emotions take us by surprise, we may be reliving our own grief. The tears we shed for others has beckoned our own pain, and we are grieving our loss once again.

Our heightened awareness of suffering can be both a blessing and a burden. While we may have become more supportive of others, we may also remain more vulnerable than we want to be.

I am aware that I have grown more tenderhearted since my loved one died. I can extend this new awareness to others who need my support and understanding. At the same time, I will stay alert to my own vulnerabilities.

The Gift of Faith

"Now faith is the substance of things hoped for, the evidence of things not seen."
Hebrews 11:1, KJ

"My eleven-year-old friend Jonathan had fought the hardest fight against cancer I had ever seen. After going through all he had endured, he still believed in God. His faith challenged not only his mother but everyone else he came in contact with. Jonathan had hoped he would beat his cancer. At times, there was evidence he was getting better. But when he no longer could see that manifested in the physical world, he kept his faith in a higher and deeper call that passed all human understanding. Jonathan continued to walk in faith. It was that faith that sustained him until the end."
Catrina Ganey, in loving memory of Jonathan.

Our loved ones leave many gifts behind when they die. These gifts are a memorial to how they lived their lives. Those like Jonathan, who chose a life of faith and hope, leave us these gifts. Their faith helps to encourage and sustain us, to remind us there is another life to hope for, even when we feel we have so little evidence of it. Faith holds us close when we grieve the loss of a loved one. It assures us that our life will continue, even in the midst of our pain.

I can think of the gifts my loved one has shared. I can call upon my own faith to sustain me, now and in the future.

Heartbreaking Memories

"One of the most heartbreaking memories of my mom's death came the night of her funeral. As I put my four young children to bed, I cried when they called me 'mommy' and said 'goodnight.' I had said 'goodnight' to my 'mommy' for the last time."

Mary Laing Kingston, to mom.

Each of us carry memories of our loved one's death that may sear our heart each time they come to mind. We shudder from their impact; we feel wounded. Yet, painful and hurtful as they are, these memories tell us of our deep love and affection for our special one. They tell us that our loved one mattered then and still matters now.

The heartbreaking memories I have of my loved one's death remind me of my deep love. I will let these memories live in me, despite the pain and hurt that can accompany them.

Death as the Door to Life

"Death is the door to life! Spiritually and emotionally, its pain, loss and silence are a central part of a 'birthing process.'"

Dr. Beverly Musgrave, in memory of her parents.

Yes, death *can* open the door to life, but we must let it happen. If we keep our grief inside, letting it ferment and stagnate, we will become as bitter as sour milk. We will be turning away from the world and all it may have to offer.

For those of us who choose to experience our pain, no matter how broken and wounded we feel, death may bring forth new life. The birth of a sense of peace from our pain will not come easy. Yet by embracing grief, we also acknowledge life, and in this embrace we find an opportunity to appreciate life anew.

I realize that the death of my loved one is an opportunity for new growth. I will carefully consider my options as I think about my grieving.

Finding Healing Through Receiving and Giving Support

"I couldn't believe that I could ever feel happy or joyful again in my life. Yet we have found healing by attending support groups, and by educating others on the treatment of depression with anti-depressants."

Mary Swanson, in loving memory of her son Brad, who was a victim of suicide.

When our grief was fresh and our loss new, it was hard to imagine that we would ever smile again or have reason to feel happy. Yet this can be possible if we are able to get the support we need and cope with our grief. Having others who share our sorrow, affirm our feelings, and listen without judging or giving unsolicited advice can be a great help to us.

The opportunity to learn from our tragedy, to help others, or do something special in tribute to our loved one can also be healing. When a positive comes from our loss, we can have good feelings in spite of our pain. Whether we plant a tree in memory of our loved one, teach others from this experience, or reach out to someone in similar pain, our contribution may bring a smile to our lips or a song to our hearts.

I can smile and be happy again. Seeking good support and honoring my loved one by helping others are just two of the paths I may take in this search for happiness and healing.

Feeling Vicitimized

"Conspiracy—it's a conspiracy. The world was picking on me today. Every single traffic light in the entire world was red, just for me. I got three hang-up calls, I picked the shortest line at the bank and waited the longest."

Darcie Sims, in loving memory of her son, Austin.

Feeling vulnerable and victimized after a crisis is common. It may seem that other people, the system, or God or a higher power is out to get us. We may start thinking that maybe there really is a conspiracy.

We may find ourselves sick, stuck in traffic, or having a day where everything goes wrong, and we may wonder, "Why me? Haven't I been through enough?"

These added pressures and problems assault our weakened body and spirit and can drain us further. When we had confidence and felt stronger, we may not have taken these things personally. Although we may be feeling vulnerable, it is helpful to keep things in perspective, even turning to humor when possible.

Even though this may be a time when I feel vulnerable, I will not let myself be brought down any further. Today I will laugh with someone, or by myself, about the irritations and problems that have recently come my way.

Appreciating Every Moment of Life

"I feel a heightened awareness of how precious life is, and how precious the people around me are. I am thankful for this."

> Vicky Campbell, in loving memory of her unborn child.

With the death of our loved one, many of us begin to realize how truly fragile and precious life is. We are painfully aware that life could end at any time, and we may regret not having appreciated every moment. Our past behavior may now disturb us.

Many of us set out to make amends. We may embrace and celebrate the family and friends we have, or, feeling a sense of urgency about life, we may try to accomplish goals long put off or set aside. Life has taken on new meaning for us, and we dare not let its preciousness slip through our fingers again.

I am reminded of how precious life is. I will not let this newfound realization slip away. Today I will remind myself of someone or something I am thankful for.

Letting Humor Balance Our Pain

*"At one point in my grieving I hit a low, overwhelmed with the conviction that my family, my neighbors, even my pets were all **old**. A friend cheerfully reminded me, 'Well, you know what all that means. **We** are older, too.' Fortunately there is humor, for it can help balance the feelings of irreplaceable loss and the perception that my family is rushing away from me."*

Colleen Kent, in memory of her family.

Grief can take such a heavy toll on our emotions that many of us may find little in life to smile or laugh about. Yet as Colleen points out, humor can offset our pain. Being overwhelmed with grief for long periods of time can lead to feelings of hopelessness, despondency, and serious depression.

The death of our loved one has left us with much to feel unhappy and miserable about. Still, a grin or a laugh may provide that important spark that brings hope and healing back into our lives.

I do not want to be overwhelmed with grief forever. I will let humor bring balance to my pain. I will let it help me find hope and healing again.

Feeling & Staying Close

"I recently went through my closet sorting out things I wanted to give away. I could have parted with almost anything but the clothing that belonged to my Mother. I wear some of her things on days I'm homesick for her. There is one particular sweater that she used to wear a lot; it still smells of her and her kitchen."

Leah Jones, in loving memory of her dear mother, Ruth.

Our loved one's belongings are permanent reminders of them. Many of us feel close once again as we touch, use, or wear their things over and over. Memories of them can come back with renewed vividness from this closeness. Wearing Grandma's wedding ring, using Dad's winter coat, or driving Sis' car are all ways of keeping our loved one with us over time, letting them become a part of us. These actions are a way to always remember, to always be close.

My loved one's belongings help me to feel close. I can find comfort in these precious reminders.

The Continuing Journey Towards Healing

Hope
by Catrina Ganey

In memory of losing a love relationship.

One must hold on to hope;
Without it,
Reasons for living become very few.
One must hold on to hope;
Even when the days are darkest,
The hours the longest,
When the heart aches the heaviest,
And promises that were made never come true,
Or are broken time and time again.
One must hold on to hope,
For without it,
There would be no need to find faith
In the midst of a situation
That is devastating!
We would not want to get out of bed in the morning,
Or dream of loving...loving...loving...
No, one must always hope.
Sometimes...
That's the only thing that keeps us alive.

Comparing Our Grief to That of Others

"My neighbor suffered a loss and seemed to be over it in six months. I don't know why it's taking me so much longer. I should be farther along by now."
Anonymous

Many of us search for a timeline to follow in moving through our grief. We may attempt to measure the intensity of our feelings and the length of time our grieving will take by comparing ourselves with others. Creating this pressure may only make things worse.

Most of us feel that we will never really "be over it," though on the outside it may look that way to others. When we love someone so much, is it possible, or wise, to stop grieving at a prescribed time? We cannot compare our emotions and needs to those of others; each of us is unique. We need to let go of trying to live up to the expectations or standards of others. Our grieving process is uniquely ours; we are where we are.

I cannot measure my emotions or grieving against someone else's. I will give myself permission to be who I am, as I am, where I am.

Is There a Purpose?

"I believe there's a purpose in why she died when she did. I feel that God picked her, a rose for His garden. I believe and trust this."

> Keith Parks, in loving memory of his first wife, Darlene.

While others may try to explain to us why our loved one has died, we alone will determine if we feel there is a purpose or a greater good that may come from this tragic event.

Some of us may believe there is a plan that is bigger than us, or that something good will come from the ashes of our loss. Others may not believe that there is a reason for our loved one's death, or we may worry that little good will come from it.

Each of us is unique, and we will believe what is within us to believe. Yet our openness to an eventual greater good—perhaps that we will become more compassionate of others—may be a comforting hope for the days ahead.

Today I can trust my beliefs about why my loved one died. I can hope that gifts will come out of the ashes of my despair.

The Pain and Joy of Memories

"Every once in awhile the door will open, and feelings will fill me; the pain and joy of their existence."

Stephen Whitman, in loving memory of his grandparents.

Months and even years after our loved one's death, we may find doors in our memory that bring us into special rooms filled with joyful or painful recollections. Sometimes the same room holds both joy and sadness.

It is possible to have both happy and sad memories at the same time. We may feel proud to have known our loved one and thankful for their lives, yet those very reminders can sting us with the sadness of missing them.

I am thankful for my loved one's specialness. I can allow both the joy and pain to coexist when those special doors open.

"Should Haves" and Regrets

"There were things we could have done after David's death, like have a special service of celebration. But we didn't. I've never regreted that decision, nor any of the others. Thankfully, we made a commitment to each other to live with our decisions and not regret what we should or could have done."

Jim Nelson, in loving memory of his son, David.

Sometimes we may dwell on the decisions we made around the time of our loved one's death. We think about what we could have or should have done, playing out each new scenario in our minds. The endless possibilities represent mysteries we can never solve.

Yet regardless of whether our decisions were ultimately the best choices or not, spending hours berating ourselves about the past is not helpful. Our regrets prevent us from living in the present, and may prolong our grieving and intensify the sadness of our loss. We need to forgive ourselves for any decisions or actions we regret, and let go of them.

I will be kind and forgiving to myself. The choices I made were the best possible decisions I could make at the time.

Carrying On a Loved One's Legacy

"I am secretly hoping that I will be able to complete some larger project that Matt would have wanted to accomplish—I don't know exactly what. I know that I want to wholeheartedly embrace those spiritual and material gifts that were left to me and to seek out some activity that I think Matt would have wanted to do. This has helped me cope with his dying. My father, mother, brother and two sisters have also gained from embracing their inheritances from Matt."

Paul Debono, in memory of his brother, Matt.

Many of us find ways to carry on the legacy of our loved one. We may finish a project that they started, or take on some of their strengths or characteristics for awhile. We might suddenly discover that we have their green thumb with plants, try one of their hobbies, or take over their role in the family. Some of us might even carry on a value or cause that was important to them. These actions help to keep their memory alive, especially within us.

I will give myself permission to be like my loved one in some way, or to find a way to carry on their legacy. I am proud of who they were, and I want to stay connected with them.

Wanting One More Chance to Be Together

"If only I could have touched my son's baby soft skin just one more time, held him a few more minutes, taken a few more pictures of him, had one more chance to say 'I love you.' Yes, I know it would never have been enough; I would always want more. We needed a lifetime to fulfill all the plans I had for him, my sweet son."

Donna Roehl, in loving memory of her son, Andrew James.

Many of us may have lingering thoughts of wanting just one more kiss, one more embrace; just a little more time together with our loved one. In our heart of hearts, however, we know that *one more* would never be enough. We could never be satisfied; there is no number that would be sufficient to quell our aching heart. The dreams and plans we had did not include a limit on our love or on the length of our life together. We expected the forever that comes with a lifetime.

It is sad to think that I will not be able to fill my need to be with the one I loved. I needed a lifetime. Today I will be grateful for the time we did have together.

Getting On With Life While Missing Them

"One must get on with life, and I have. I am happy, and life is good; but when I sit looking through my junk drawer with all its memories, I think of how much I loved my brother and how much he meant to me. The tears come freely. I miss him."

> *Mark D. Rittmann, in loving memory of his brother and friend, Roger.*

Most of us find a way of going on after our loved one dies, painful as some days might be. Still, getting on with life does not mean that our sorrow magically ends, or that we stop loving and missing them. Memories of the life we shared and all that the past held will always touch our heart. As happy as our life may become, the missing and the longing linger, and never quite end.

Although I am moving on with life, memories wash over me from time to time and bring my loved one back. I miss my loved one.

Finding Relief Through Crying

"Tears help wash away the pain. Tears are good to release my feelings of pain and loneliness. Even our Lord wept at the death of a close friend. He understands my pain and gives me hope for today and the future. My life will go on, but my memory of Jeff will last forever."

Barbara Arndt Hampson, in memory of her son, Jeff Arndt.

Sometimes it's good to cry, to let out the feelings hidden in our heart and soul that we're too afraid or fragile to show. The feelings we fear won't ever stop.

By crying, we set our feelings free. Free to find resolution, understanding, or peace. Just as a twig winds it way down a stream in the spring, so too feelings of pain and desolation can float away with our tears.

I will let myself cry from time to time and I won't try to stop it. I can feel good after these times, enjoying the relief that crying brings.

New Perspectives On Past Differences

"I have learned that there is beauty everywhere—in the most unexpected places—if I look for it. I had disliked my son's friends, but after he died, we discovered that we needed each other. Now some of them come regularly to visit, and we talk and play games, eat supper together, and share memories. How I wish my son were here to share these times with us, to see how my eyes have been opened to so many things."

Karen Grover, in loving memory of her son, David.

There may have been a number of things that we didn't like about our loved one's life. Their attitudes, choice of activities, or lifestyle may not have suited us. But unexpectedly, we may find ourselves understanding just a bit more about our loved one's choices, and we may feel more of a need to be close with them, despite our differences.

It may be sad to think that we missed having a better relationship because of past differences or disagreements. Karen opened her eyes, seeing beauty where she had once only felt distain. We, too, can try to forgive ourselves and be open to the beauty that change can bring.

I can feel both regret and happiness about the unexpected discoveries that have come to me since my loved one died. I can accept and appreciate this new perspective.

Sharing a Special Experience

"Today I saw two deer running through the yard. My first thought was that I wanted to share the sight with my Grandmother. She always got excited when she saw deer. Perhaps her spirit was present, sharing the moment with me."

Sherokee Ilse, in loving memory of Gram Kriesch.

There will be moments all through our lives when we feel close to our loved one who has died, especially when there is an experience we wish we could share with them. We may feel the urge to call them, write to them, or visit them. Although these feelings may bring frustration and sadness, we can look at it from another angle. This special event or moment is more memorable because of our loved one. They are near us in heart and mind. We are sharing the experience with them, and they with us.

When a special moment or experience reminds me of my loved one, I will embrace it. I can feel that my loved one is sharing it with me, and be thankful for that.

The Prayers of Others

"I truly believe my recovery was dependent largely on my friends' prayers. Letter after letter assured me, 'We're praying for you.'"

Dorothy Hsu, in memory of her husband, Min.

Like Dorothy, many of us believe that prayer has played a vital part in our healing. We may feel reassured knowing that others have spoken to God on our behalf. Their prayers bring us comfort and a sense of peacefulness. Knowing that others care enough to pray can give us hope, and help us realize how important we are to them. The thoughtfulness and prayers of our friends may give us the courage to believe that we can survive. And we are surviving.

I appreciate the prayers and thoughtfulness of my friends. I will thank them for praying on my behalf.

Bitter Grief

"It helped me to believe that bitter grief could not poison the sweetness of my grandchild's time."
Anonymous

The taste and experience of grief can be painfully bitter. The bitterness may lead some of us to get caught up in fighting the grief; we want to avoid the journey altogether. Others of us become so consumed by grief that we lose sight of this special person and their gifts.

As we mourn, we can remind ourselves to appreciate the sweetness of our loved ones, what made them special and unique. We can remember why we love them, even in the midst of our grieving or our avoidance.

I will not allow my grief and sorrow to poison my memories and love. I can try to control this with a positive attitude.

Hope Begins to Emerge

"Without the valleys there would be no mountain. And if you don't scale the mountain, you won't see the view."
Anonymous

Most of us want to experience the happiness, the emotional peaks, the "spectacular views" in life. Yet we may try to avoid the valleys, afraid of the depth of pain and anguish they may bring.

Having been in the valley, usually not by choice, most of us come to a time where we have struggled up a hill and are amazed by the view; the beauty fills us, and we are thankful for having made it this far. Amazingly, hope emerges. There may have been many days when making this climb was impossible to imagine.

This emerging hope reminds us that life has its beauty; there are things to live for, to look forward to. Looking back down at the valley and the long, dark journey helps us to feel grateful that we are now rarely at such low points. We are getting better. There is hope.

Though the struggle from the valley has not been easy, I can accept the hope that emerges. I can appreciate the view.

Recurring Dreams

"Though my lover is dead,
we meet in my dreams.
Dreams so real they stir me from sleep,
rekindling that awful ache
as I sit trembling on the edge of my empty bed."

> *Robert Krisch, in loving memory of his wife, Kathy, who died one day after giving birth to their fourth child.*

The dreams we have of our loved one can be both reassuring and unnerving. We can feel comforted by once again seeing the one we love as we drift off to a faraway land. And yet, awakening from our dreams can rudely disrupt our peacefulness and badly disorient us as we ache for their presence and touch. It can be difficult and disturbing to try to reconcile these opposing worlds.

Dreams often reflect our inner wishes. The longing we continue to feel for our loved one can easily slip into our nighttime thoughts. As we come closer to accepting our loved one's death, we may find our dreams reflecting our healing as well.

I can focus on the good sensations and feelings that come when I dream of my loved one. I need not be afraid of the thoughts that enter my slumber.

Growth From Our Sorrow

"At least two important things have come out of my loss experience. I have been able to help others who experience the loss of a child because I now understand and can emphathize with them. Also, I feel I am a much more compassionate person."

Lisa Strother, in memory of her precious son, John Mark, Jr. "I knew you only briefly, but will remember you for a lifetime."

Does anything good come from the grief over a loved one's death? There may have been many times when our answer would have been an emphatic "No!" We may have wondered why we should even consider the idea that something positive could result. After all, the pain was so intense, the tunnel so dark...we may not have been able to believe that there could ever be a good side. Such doubts might still exist.

In time, as we grieve and heal, it is possible to see light in the tunnel, to have positive thoughts, and to find patches of hope in this nightmare. We may realize we have changed, like Lisa has. We may look at life differently, recognizing the fragility of life and even gaining new appreciation for the miracles of birth and nature, for good health, or valued relationships.

Today I will think of one or two things that have happened since my loved one's death that I feel good about. I will remind myself of a way that I have grown or have had a change in perspective.

Lingering Resentment

"I'm ashamed to say I can never forget one particular friend who said she "knew" how I felt, yet didn't have the slightest clue. My head tells me to let it go, because she meant well. My heart holds on tight to a resentment so bitter I can taste it, even a long time later."

Marie Radtke Teague, in loving memory of her son, Brian Christopher.

We may not want to admit it, but we still may resent the actions or comments made by a number of people at the time of our loved one's death. Maybe their comments were painful, or they gave us inappropriate advice, or completely ignored us.

These feelings add to our pain, yet they may often be unavoidable. Our anger and disappointment can be hard to put aside. Still, while working towards forgiveness may not be easy, it can be quite healing. Through prayer, putting our feelings on paper, or some other method, we can attempt to forgive them, and then move on.

Resentment and disappointment are valid feelings. Yet to help myself heal, I can bring forgiving thoughts to the surface today.

Time Becomes a Friend

"Time cannot steal the precious memories that we carry in our hearts."

Diana and Mark Sundwall, in loving memory of their son, Derek.

Time, often perceived as an enemy in the early days of our grief, can become a friend later on. We need not fear it any longer.

There may have been a point in our journey when we waited for time to dull our pain and even the memories which brought the pain. Later on, we may have actually *feared* that our memories of our loved one would drift away over time, leaving us without a clear picture of their lives and what they mean to us.

Now we see that we have survived and that we continue to carry our special memories of our loved one. Time can be a friend, reminding us that it will preserve our memories forever.

I need not fear time any longer. It can become a dependable friend, reminding me I will always cherish my memories.

Feeling Confidence

"The death of my sons has taught me that good can come from tragedy if one looks for a way. I discovered that my anger could be channeled into energy, and that energy could be used for good. I live with hope in my heart for a better tomorrow and a deep faith in my God, the God that I was once so angry with. I know now that I can do many things that I once thought impossible."

> *Betty Jane Spencer, in loving memory of her four sons who were murdered.*

Trying to survive the death of our loved one has presented us with many challenges, some of which seemed impossible to overcome at one time. Many of us were burdened by a lack of confidence and low self-worth. Few of us felt prepared—emotionally, physically, or spiritually—for what was ahead.

For many, gaining through adversity and finding ways to turn our tragedy into good helps to buoy our confidence. Our strengthened feelings can help us to find hope in life and perhaps even enrich our relationship with God. Feeling confident and able to succeed over life's challenges is reassuring. These feelings help us to see that what once seemed impossible *is* possible. We can learn many things as we work to survive the death of our loved one.

Though I may have been lacking in confidence at different times, I can see that this experience has helped to build and strengthen my self-worth. I can now see possibilities where I only saw impossibilities.

Pressures to Be "Better"

"The pressures to be competent and 'all better' at work, at home, and even among my friends is more than I can bear sometimes. They expect me to be upbeat and confident, yet there are still many days when I just can't put on a happy face or do the tasks I need to do."

Anonymous

Outside pressures combined with our internal pressures often push us to be "better" quicker than our mind and body really can. Some of us may have jumped back into work soon after the crisis and sped along on the fast track for many months. At times we may have felt quite confident and strong. Still, a time may finally come when we stop and ask ourselves, "What's going on?" We may find ourselves feeling distant, tearful, and quite low. This may be a sign that we need some space, rest, and time to heal.

We have changed significantly inside. Except for close friends and relatives, others may not see our insecurities and anguish. Instead, they may see us functioning fairly well, believing we have put thoughts of our loved one's death behind us for the most part. Although friends, relatives, co-workers, and even our boss may expect us to perform at old levels, this may be extremely difficult given our fluctuating emotions. Being aware of the pressures and releasing them from time to time can help.

I am still healing. I will do my best to keep the pressure to a minimum. When I feel it is necessary, I will let those who are putting too much pressure on me know how difficult it is for me.

Envy and Jealousy of Others

"I look at others who have complete families and I feel so jealous. I miss my parents. I feel like an orphan, abandoned, even though I'm no longer a child."

Sondra Kingsbury, in loving memory of her mom and dad.

When someone is missing in our lives we may feel envious and jealous that others have what we don't, their parents, children, siblings—their loved ones. Though we do not wish such a loss on them, we are reminded that our loved one's death has left a void, and we are pained. Sadly, their fortune points out our misfortune.

It may be helpful to simply accept our feelings and not feel guilty about having them. If we are honest about our reactions, and perhaps share them with others, our envy and jealousy may decrease over time.

When I do feel envious or jealous of others, I can accept these feelings as natural responses to my loneliness and pain.

Empowered To Go On

"My family and I survived because we believe in tomorrow."

Rhonda Hufman, in loving memory of Emma and Joe Hufman, and Florence and Bill Gannon.

Our motivation to survive the death of our loved one is as unique as our fingerprint. Some of us may have turned to our faith or our friends to give us support and encouragement; others of us may have drawn upon our own inner resources to give us strength. No matter what has enabled us to go on and face our pain and devastation, we are all miraculously surviving the loss of our loved one. Time has helped heal our brokenness, and the joys of life have allowed our hearts to open again. We have been empowered to go on.

I am empowered to survive the loss of my loved one. I can celebrate the future I have to live.

Drawing Inspiration From
Our Loved One's Life

"His carefree ways have inspired me to live a freer life. 'Carpe diem' (seize the day) has become the motto of my life. Live life to its fullest, that's what Rich did."

> *Michelle Dubreuil, in loving memory of her brother, Rich.*

There may be aspects of our loved one's life that we want to carry on or incorporate into our own lives. Learning to play the same musical instrument, adopting their concern for a special issue, or taking up one of their hobbies are all different ways of doing this. By emulating our loved one, we honor them and help them to live on in us. In this way, we can carry on the unique and wonderful spirit of our loved one.

Though my loved one has died, I can let their spirit live on in the world. I can cherish and carry on an aspect of their unique life.

Still Struggling With Acceptance

"With our son's death, our world felt like it collapsed. I have tried to fit this terrible destruction of our lives into a place that I can understand. We are Christians, yet I find all this so hard to accept. My head and my heart do not want to agree."

> Nina Nesbit, in memory of her son, Stanley Wayne.

Many of us still struggle to accept our loved one's death. We have tried to believe what has happened, but we can't quite reconcile reality with our emotions. We long to have our loved one back. Accepting that they are gone forever, never to be a living part of our world again, can still feel overwhelming.

Our clash between our heads and hearts may put us in a sort of limbo. We continue to have trouble accepting that our loved one is gone forever, yet we know that they are dead. We may feel trapped, uncertain of how to resolve our inner conflict.

In order to move on and return to life, we need to slowly let our loved one go. We need to accept that they will not return to this life. We can trust that it is not necessary for us to have all the answers in order to move on.

There are times when my heart struggles to accept the realities of my loved one's death. I still long for the company of the one I loved. I don't want to be trapped in limbo forever, and when I'm ready, I will let my loved one go, if but a little at a time.

Gathering Memories

"Good memories are the perennials that bloom again after the hard winter of grief begins to yield to hope."
   sascha

The intense winter of our grief is a very lonely and difficult time. Special memories of our loved one soften the harshness and warm us. Spring presents itself tentatively at first, bringing with it the flowering reminders of our loved one. These memories give us hope. We are surviving.

We may crave each and every memory of our loved one. As we relive them and share them, the spring of our grief brings out the sun, the colors, the flowers of today, and the hope of tomorrow.

In my gathering of memories I will invite courage to help me remember everything, as I move from winter to spring.

Approaching the Anniversary

"Many days have passed since he left. The weeks flew by, and it is now getting close to that time of year that is both sad, yet joyful: the anniversary. It is so hard to let go fully."

Suzanne Knopf, in loving memory of her son, Jamieson Sean.

The days before the anniversary of a loved one's death can be an anxious and sometimes stressful time. We may look back on this as the longest year of our lives, or it may seem hard to believe that a year has almost come and gone. We may recall the violent pain as if it were only yesterday. Seeking to put an entire year behind us, we may have tried to wish time away. Now that it is almost upon us, we may scarcely be able to believe it.

At this time, the joy and sadness of our loved one's life and death often combine and bring forth deep emotions. We can find ourselves more tearful, angry, or especially sensitive. We wonder if we should try to put all this behind us as we prepare to begin a new year.

Although a year is significant, it is not the end of grieving or the automatic beginning of a new, happy life. Nor is it something to fear. It may be a turning point. For many of us, it may mean we survived longer than we thought we could. Soon we head into the second cycle of everything; the second Memorial Day, Thanksgiving, holiday season, Mother and Father's Day, and other significant occasions.

I will allow myself to feel the pain and the joy of the upcoming anniversary of my loved one's death. I need not fear this day, but can feel hopeful about it.

Life Has Promise

"It seems strange, but now I sense that life may hold some promise. My brother is still dead, and my love for him has not lessened. But I am not as consumed by my grief. I feel the buddings of a new life; new dreams, goals, and challenges. I feel freer to engage in life again and to pursue the future that beckons me."

Elsa Larson, in memory of her brother, Harold Bueide Haaland.

Early in our grief, many of us could not have imagined that life would hold promise again. Surviving from one week to the next, or even day to day may have been more than we could bear at times. We were consumed by heartache and pain for the one we loved.

Yet there may be days now when thinking about the future and planning ahead seems possible. Having come closer to accepting our loved one's death as a reality, we can now allow ourselves some freedom to think beyond the immediate. We may now believe there will be a tomorrow. Pursuing life again may seem to make sense.

I can think about the future. Life may hold promise for me again, if I will just pursue it.

Pressure to Put Away Mementos

"I don't understand why people pressure me to take down the pictures and mementos of my 'daddy.' I'll always love him, and I want those reminders surrounding me."

    Connie Lindsley Espinoza, in loving memory of her earthly "daddy," Verlin "Jim" Lindsley.

Many of us feel these same pressures. We may be told directly or given hints that these reminders of our loved one ought to be put away, especially after so much time. These symbols may remind our friends and family of our sorrow and heartache, as well as their own pain. They may simply be feeling uncomfortable and want us to move on, thinking that this is the best way for us to be happy again. But our feelings may be quite different.

We do not have to put away the pictures and mementos. We love that person; they are still a member of our family, still important to us. The tears and the joy which spring forth from our loved one's keepsakes may bring us comfort.

If we follow the advice of others against our better judgment, we may notice that it doesn't feel quite right. It is wise to trust our inner sense of what we need to do.

I will trust my judgment about keeping the reminders of my loved one around me.

I'm So Glad You Came
by Jane Peterson

In memory of her daughter,
Colleen Kryder Murphy.

I'm so glad you came
For I will always know your light
In my hands;
Always.

And the power of your leaving
Was exquisite.
A kind of profound silence.
I will always be able to recall it
In a moment;
Always.

But I am so glad you came.
So incredibly honored
To have known you at all.
I will always know your light
In my hands,
And in a blink, I will see it;
Always.

The Continuing Journey Towards Healing

Change and Rebirth

"I have found that grief is really an exchange. I died in a way when Jesse died, but I also came back to life with keener insights, with compassion for others in pain, and with a deeper sense of self. Jesse's birth spawned my rebirth. It doesn't make up for my intense loss, but it does add a new dimension to me. I am happy again."

     Susan Erling, in memory of her stillborn son, Jesse.

Many of us believe that when our loved one died, part of us died as well. We may see this as the death of our old self, happy self, or comfortable self. And just as trees shed their leaves in the fall, a part of us no longer exists. Yet, amazingly, that part of us that died allows something new to grow in its place. Susan describes this as an exchange; a rebirth. As we heal, we may develop a strengthened sense of self, a renewed appreciation for nature, or a fresh outlook on life. Though it may not be possible to measure what we have lost, new life has been brought forth.

While a part of me died with my loved one, I am grateful for all that my rebirth has brought. Today I will spend some time thinking about the changes —the exchanges—that I have made.

Lingering Disbelief

"There are still some days when I can't believe my mother really died. Even though much time has passed, I still start to call her when I have some special news. She really died, didn't she?"

> Linda Hall Whitman, in loving memory of her mother.

For months we may go along believing that we have accepted the fact that our loved one has died. Then one day we want to see them or talk to them, and it hits us again. They really aren't here!

It seems like only yesterday that they were with us, yet the calendar shows how much time has really passed. Our heart's denial of their death may surprise us, yet it is real and even appropriate. There is no timetable or prescription to grieving.

Healing and accepting my loved one's death takes time. When I have moments of denial or disbelief, I can free myself from a prescribed timetable and allow myself to follow my heart.

Recognition of Our Adjustments

"Oh, I can function again. I laugh freely. I've learned new skills, like making out my income tax and pumping gas at the self-serve station. I've had a date and would even welcome marriage again should the right person ask me. But my husband is still a part of my life—he is tucked away safely and permanently in my heart."

Dorothy Hsu, in memory of her very special companion, her husband, Min.

There comes a time for many of us when we can step back and feel pleased about the adjustments we have made since our loved one's death. We may have acquired new skills, made modifications in our lifestyle, or allowed ourselves to think seriously about the future. Though our wounds may have been slow to mend, these changes record our healing and growth.

Trying to adjust to our loved one's death has not been easy, nor has it come quickly. As we continue to heal, the memory of our loved one burns vivid and bright.

I feel good about the adjustments that I have made in my life. I am continuing to heal and grow. Memories of my loved one are an important part of me.

Reorganizing Our Lives

"Somehow a spell was broken, and I woke up one day wanting to be alive again. We are able to laugh and play again."

Tree Johnson, in loving memory of her husband, Bruce, who was killed in a car accident.

As we move toward reorganizing our lives, we need to find ways to incorporate our feelings and memories of our loved one into who we are today. Their life and death has changed us. We go on, with a new order to our days and a new view of the world.

We can find ways to work, be social, carry on with our responsibilities, and even laugh and play at times. Yet as we move toward happiness and the good feeling of wanting to be alive again, we will continue to find ways of remembering our special person.

As I move towards living life fully, I will let my laughter and playfulness come out.

Surviving

"Since Lloyd's death, I have learned I can survive. I've learned my world is different now, but I can make it better because of the deep love my son and I shared and still share."

Norma Long Wood

When we look back wistfully over the past months, most of us can take pride in seeing that we have survived our loved one's death. There may have been many times when we doubted that we had either the will or the ability to survive. Our road was unfamiliar and strewn with obstacles; there was little sun to light our way. Yet despite the difficulties, we found both the strength and tools to survive. We learned how to push aside the obstacles and find our way in the darkness.

Our loved one's death created a different world for us. And, as the world changed, so have we. We have learned to survive.

I can accept that my world has changed since my loved one died. I have changed, too. I can take pride in seeing that I have survived.

Feeling Discouraged

"I thought I'd be done with this grieving by now. It takes so much work, and it's so painful. It's so discouraging when those dark days come. Why can't I just be happy again?"

> *Sheryl Boman, in loving memory of her father, Donald.*

After months of grieving, with all its ups and downs, we may find ourselves feeling discouraged at times. Experiencing the anguish and sorrow over and over again may have become tiring. It's natural to want to "be done," to move on and feel healed. We may wonder if we have been doing something wrong, or if there is something wrong with us. Yet, grieving cannot be so easily controlled. It is bigger than us, and a much longer process than we might think.

The storm of grief following death does last a long time. We may hope for calm and peaceful seas, yet in our hearts we know that a windy day or a raging storm may be around any corner. Our love for this special person means that we are forever bound to them. As time goes on we may have many more calm days than stormy, but we need to be aware that storms and windy days are a part of the natural cycle of life, not to be avoided but to be weathered.

On my calm days I will relish the peace and gain strength for the stormy days that will arise now and again.

Adapting

"I liken my grief to the bird with a broken wing. She never soared so high again, but her song was so much sweeter."
Karen McGivney-Liechti, in loving memory of Neil McGivney, Monte Brecht, and Nicholas Brecht Liechti.

Wounded and unable to fly as she once did, the bird adapted to life by developing a sweeter song. She focused her efforts on that over which she had some control; her voice. In the same way, our woundedness and our grief has encouraged many of us to adapt in new and different ways to our changed world.

In coping with our loved one's death, we may have sought to develop forgotten skills or abilities, faced ultimate fears, or adopted new ways of living. As we continue to integrate and incorporate these changes into our lives, we can feel encouraged by our ability to adapt and grow.

The bird triumphed over adversity, and so it is with me. From the depths of my sorrow I can learn to adapt.

Peace and Serenity

"My peace and serenity has returned; I feel reborn. I can live each day of my life as a prayer."
Mayrse Wilde, in memory of her son, Ricky-Adrian.

To reinvest in life, to have another child, to love again, or to find peace and serenity are goals that each of us has had throughout the difficult times. At some moments those goals seem unattainable, as if they are part of a far away galaxy, light years from us. Yet, through the work of grief, and with support and the comfort of memories, it is possible to touch those places of peace, to seek new love, and to reinvest in living.

Serenity and peace can come. When they do, we need to embrace them and revel in the healing that has taken place. At the same time, we can recognize that we have changed. We carry our loved one within us.

I can seek peace and serenity. I can begin to feel ready to love again, to risk that part of me that fears I will suffer again. I will revel in the peace and serenity when it touches me.

Living Life Again

"This life we take for granted
Is really very fragile.
Live it with exuberance!
Let thankfulness flow through you.
Welcome the sunshine and the rain.
Share the smiles and the pain.
Be grateful for every breath you take
Because life is God's most precious gift—
Make no mistake."

       Betty Stallings, from the dedication of a memorial bench for her son, David, at Dry Creek Elementary School.

Living life again does not come easy for many of us. It may be a long, lonely journey marked by many disappointments. Yet, wonderment may be found along the way as well. Living again means accepting life's intensity, respecting its fragility and its force, and experiencing its immense beauty and grotesque ugliness. Life is a precious gift; maybe one that can only be fully appreciated by those who have faced the grimness of death and found hope.

Today I can welcome life—sunshine and rain, laughter and pain. Life is a precious gift for which I am grateful.

Gifts and Empowerment Provided
by Our Loved Ones

"My Dad left me so many gifts and good memories. He taught me to accept both love and death through his example. His support and faith in my ability to deal directly with my Aunt Rosa's dying and death when I was just thirteen typified his love for life and those who loved him."

Dick Friberg, in memory of his father, Roy C. Friberg.

Dick's father enriched and deepened his life. Acting as an example, Roy empowered his son to both brave the adversities and appreciate the goodness life has to offer. Dick is grateful for the gifts and memories his father gave him.

In their own ways, our loved ones have also empowered us. We may have gained from their wisdom, their genuine love for us, their very presence in our lives. Our memories will forever remind us of all we have learned from them. We can be eternally thankful for our loved one.

I am grateful for the presence of my loved one in my life. The gifts and memories that they have given me are a tribute to their existence.

Coming Together Again

"I found that healing is like assembling a puzzle, beginning at its center and building outwards without knowledge of a border or ending. As the scene develops, the intensity softens—the healing proceeds."

Anonymous

The death of our loved one left many of us feeling like we'd been fractured into hundreds of unconnected pieces. Like tiny parts of a difficult puzzle, the fragments of our life had to be fitted together again. We may still need to be made whole. We still need to heal.

To assemble this puzzle meant facing the unknowns and uncertainties of our shattered lives. We had to sort through the scrambled pieces, looking for a sense of order and meaning. These tasks took much effort and called us to adapt and change. As we tried to carefully put the puzzle together, healing has taken place.

Life has felt scrambled, like hundreds of pieces in a puzzle. I have worked hard to reconstruct and rebuild my life and to put this puzzle together. It may not yet be complete, but I have healed and will continue to heal.

Bad Days

"For awhile I just stuffed the urge to grieve... Now I let it happen. It doesn't happen as often now, and somehow I feel a sense of closeness...and there is a cleansing that goes along with the pain."
    Jill Cerulli

The bad days never quite leave us completely. Like a sudden rainshower in the middle of a sunny day, our urge to grieve can seem to come out of nowhere. We may see a cherished memento, find a favored piece of clothing, or hear a once familiar melody and gasp from a sudden stab of pain. Once again we miss our loved one terribly.

Usually the bad days or moments seem to leave as quickly as they came. And like the rainbow that follows the storm, the aftereffects of our grief may possess a splendid surprise; we may feel closer and more intimate with our loved one.

I will have bad days from time to time. I will not fear these days, nor hide from my need to grieve. I will let my feelings flow freely and cherish the closeness and cleansing that will follow.

Peacefulness

"Nothing can bring you peace but yourself."
Ralph Waldo Emerson

Often our desire to get on with life is intertwined with our own sense of peacefulness. For many, the extreme pain we once felt is now diminishing, and we are feeling better about the world and our place in it. We can replace the anger, envy, and rage that once over-powered us with acceptance and relief. Our attention may now be focused away from the world we once saw as so hostile and foreign.

Our sense of peacefulness comes slowly. We may recognize the genuine beauty in a patchwork quilt, experience the joy of a true friend, or relish a playful moment with a family member. These simple pleasures can bring us into harmony with those around us and in accord with the world.

The sense of peace I need is inside me. As I draw it out, I can feel better about my life and the world I am a part of. I will feel encouraged to enter life again.

Feeling Envious

"I hated seeing other women laughing and holding hands with their husbands. I was angry when I heard wives or girlfriends complain about their partners. I was envious and so jealous. My husband was dead. I couldn't hold his hand, or laugh with him. How dare those women complain, I thought. At least they have a man to love."

Anonymous

There may be times in our grief when we envy what everyone seems to have but us. Others can watch their children grow, get advice from their dad, or have someone with whom they can share their affection. The differences between what they have and what we have can feel enormous.

As our tolerance for this disparity grows thin, we may find ourselves angry and resentful of others. We want what they have. We want our loved one back. The thought that our life has changed and our dreams evaporated can be disheartening.

Yet feeling envious of others can keep us from enjoying the life we do have. Life is not fair. Comparing ourselves to others and focusing on what we're missing keeps us from seeing today and all it promises.

When I feel envious or jealous of others, I will think about what I'm missing or wanting. I will not let my envy keep me from enjoying the life I have.

Increased Empathy

"Blessed are they that mourn: for they shall be comforted."
Matthew 5:4, KJ

Our loss experience can give us the ability to better empathize with and comfort others. Having lived with the pain of a miscarriage, lengthy illness, or sudden death, we come to have a greater appreciation for the important task of giving genuine comfort and support to others.

The word "comfort" comes from the Greek PARA, which means "beside, or alongside" and KALEO, "to call." Comfort, then, means to be called alongside. Knowing how to comfort others, walking with them, is something we now understand.

Reaching out to others through community work or other volunteer activities provides opportunities where we can use our experience of loss to help others. To give in these ways honors our loved one and returns some of the care that was given us in our desperate time of need.

I can share the comfort that was freely given to me. Today I will bring a little sunshine into someone's life.

Lingering Feelings of Emptiness

"Though I've gone on with life, I still wait for the phone to ring and the sound of my grandma's voice, or think that she'll knock on my door and give me a warm hug. I look at pictures of us all and I can't believe I'll never see her again. I feel so alone. I miss her. I wish she was here. I want her back."

Suzanne Brammeier, in loving memory of her grandmother, Agnes Sutton.

The emptiness we feel from knowing that we can't share our life with our loved one may still be excruciating. We want to be with them; touch them, talk with them. Their presence gave meaning to our life, and without them we feel isolated and alone. We are haunted by the many things we can no longer share. Reinvesting in life, in our job or other activities, may have helped to lessen our pain. Yet, we still hunger for the companionship of our loved one. No longer being able to share life as we did has created a hole in our heart.

Though time has passed, I still feel empty knowing I can't share my life with my loved one. I can give myself permission to miss them.

Anniversary Anxiety

"I can't begin to describe the amount of apprehension and dread my husband and I experienced in anticipation of the first anniversary of our grandchild's death. We had no idea how to make this day easier on us."

Anonymous

As the anniversary date of our loved one's death approaches many of us become filled with anxiety and tension. We fear having to face that dreadful day and all the reminders associated with it. We want to banish it from the calendar forever, but we know we cannot. Finding a way to get through this difficult day may be uppermost in our mind.

It is normal to feel anxious and apprehensive about our loved one's anniversary date. There are far too many painful memories tied to it. As with many other things in life, though, our worrying and fretting may prove to be more distressing than the actual day. Planning how to spend the time and focusing on the good in our life may be of some help in trying to cope with this troubling time.

It is okay if I feel some apprehension or fear at the impending anniversary of my loved one's death. I can think of how I want to spend the time and make the day easier on me.

Memories Becoming a Source of Joy

"It's been weeks since I thought about my father. When I do, however, it's no longer an insurmountable pain. Now it is a deep sadness of missing him, mixed with the great joy of keeping him in my heart forever."

Kate Moore, in loving memory of her father, Wilbur.

There may be periods from time to time when we don't think about our loved one as much. Yet when we do bring them back to mind, we may find ourselves smiling, thinking happy thoughts, rather than crying or feeling sad. We have come a long way in our grief.

This doesn't mean we have forgotten our loved one, or that they aren't important to us any longer. We have learned to let go a little, realizing that the pain need not consume our daily thoughts and lives. Still, there is no doubt that they are in our hearts forever. We are weaving them into the fabric of our lives, and we needn't remind ourselves to think of them every day.

I will weave my loved one into the fabric of my life. It's okay not to think about them all the time; my love for them will still shine through.

The Intensity of the First Year

"The whole first year was exaggerated, extreme, and intense. Every thought was monumental, every action thought out thoroughly. And I cried gallons of tears."

Maggie Merkow, in loving memory of her husband, Rob.

Grief is an emotional rollercoaster which challenges and changes us. Looking back over the year, we may wonder how we have made it this far. We have seen the deep lows, dips, and even the emotional peaks, noticing their extremes. The uncontrollable days of confusion, anger, and pain have been balanced by the accepting, calmer days. We can feel thankfulness and a sense of accomplishment at having coped so well.

Getting that year behind us will be a big milestone. Though the intense feelings will continue to come and go, hopefully the drastic peaks and valleys of the rollercoaster will level somewhat. We can go on from here.

I have survived almost a year of intense grieving. I can feel proud and thankful, trusting that I will have strength in the new year to come.

Appreciating Our Loved One's Life

"Losing my parents was devastating. Later, when the silence allowed a small, gentle flow of music to return to my heart, then and only then could I experience the depth of gratitude, appreciation, and pride for the richness of their lives."

Dr. Beverly Musgrave, in loving memory of her parents, Mr. & Mrs. Fred P. Musgrave.

Our devastating pain and sorrow can be so over-whelming that they obscure the beauty of our loved one's life. Enveloped in mourning, we need calmness and quiet to reclaim their life. We have much to appreciate, and as the pain subsides, thoughts of gratitude and pride will find their way to our heart.

Though I may have temporarily lost sight of my loved one's contributions to life, I can rediscover those gifts. Today I will spend a few moments remembering my loved one's specialness.

Death As A Teacher

"My Mom's death taught me the value of gratitude and the necessity of expressing it regularly. As a result, my relationship with my father has been immeasurably strengthened. Now I make a point of calling regularly just to tell him I love him and I'm thinking about him."

Al Honrath, in memory of his mother, Rose Kerkvliet Honrath.

Death is a great teacher. From death we learn to value and appreciate life, to be more genuine with those we love, and to be grateful for the life we have. While these lessons were learned during our darkest hour, they have brought a priceless gift: embracing life and all it holds.

From my grief, precious gifts of life have come. I can accept these gifts gratefully.

Homesickness

"Often, the tears I shed for my mom were tears of homesickness, tears of longing."

Leah Jones, in loving memory of her mother, Ruth, whose death came all too soon.

Missing our loved one and longing for them never completely ends. We can feel homesick for them at a family gathering, or when we see others enjoying themselves. A favorite song or special flower can trigger our yearning. We will always miss our loved one. Nothing can quite replace the specialness and closeness we shared. For all its sadness, a twinge of homesickness might always follow us.

The absence of my loved one may leave me homesick. I miss them and long for their closeness. My tears are a sign of my yearning.

Beyond The First Year

Feeling The Loss
*by Gisela Schubach, in memory of all those
who live in her thoughts.*

Bewilderment—
exhaustion—
loneliness—
emptiness—
feeling a void in your life—
feeling abandoned—
fear of the future—
feeling of relief—
remorse—
feeling you don't want to live anymore either—
hopelessness—
physical weakness—

Guilt:
guilt when you smile again—laugh again
guilt when you start forgetting
guilt that you have the desire to live again
guilt that you get hungry and need other people

Memories and more pain—
someone else loses a loved one and everything comes
   back again—
the feeling that the pain will never end—
a Christmas that breaks your heart
a day when you cry all day long.

And then—one day—
you smile when you remember
your heart opens up for things around you
you plan new endeavors
you rationalize:
you tell yourself you are a fool to put so much love in
   one person—

you tell yourself it is okay, you will survive—
the memories become more wonderful
you tell yourself you were fortunate to have felt so much
you reach out and hold a hand that may need it more
   than you do.
you see the world again and it fills you with joy!
you philosophize:
my own life will one day be memories only—to others
you go on.

Risking New Beginnings

"It's a risk to attempt new beginnings. Yet the greater risk is for you to risk nothing. For there will be no further possibilities of learning and changing, of traveling upon the journey of life. You were strong to hold on. You will be stronger to go forward to new beginnings."

*from **Time Remembered: A Journal for Survivors** by Rabbi Dr. Earl A. Grollman.*

When we love someone, we risk being hurt. When we cry, we risk appearing weak. When we move forward, we risk failure. Yet if we don't dare to get close to people, make commitments, or take new paths, we deprive ourselves not only of the pain of life, but also the joys, the growth, and the challenge.

We need to dare ourselves to move ahead, to walk into the future with our heads held high and our hopes strong. We have survived life's journey so far; now we must find the courage to seek and build our new beginnings.

I will find the courage to risk a new beginning today, to try out a new behavior, change my attitude, or develop a new interest.

Renewed Hope and Faith

"I have cried my tears
I have asked my whys
I have mourned the future that may not be
I have planted my hope in the God who made me
He is my refuge in this storm"

> *Betty Stallings, in loving memory of her sweet child, David.*

The time does come when we feel that most of our tears have been shed and our whys asked. Our longing for all that will not be is now seeded by fresh dreams. Out of our despair, we have found a sense of hope. For some, this hope lies in God. Others find it in a renewed appreciation of nature, or a thankfulness for life.

Moving on is a challenge. Hope can come from letting go of much of our intense pain, from accepting reality, and from new dreams. While our tears may still come and the "whys" still find their way to our lips, our faith and hope for the future can be the firm footing we need to go forward.

As my tears subside and the whys fade away, I can find hope. I do not have to understand all that has happened. Both faith and hope can be a refuge.

Feeling Whole Again

"Will I ever feel whole again? Sometimes I wonder."
　　　Sheryl Boman, in loving memory of her father,
Donald.

We feel so broken and confused for such a long time after our loved one dies. That brokenness may almost seem to have become a part of our personality. From time to time we may still fade off into remembering, cry when discussing parenthood or childhood, or feel confused over issues or decisions that relate to our loved one and our family. It is natural to wish for the wholeness of the past and yet worry that we will never be whole again.

Wholeness can come, although not always as fast as we might wish. It is a long process that slowly brings us to the point where we may come to say, "Mostly, I feel happy and whole again." This new wholeness incorporates our loved one, their death, our healing, and our changed outlook on life. We need to trust that we are on the way to being whole again, perhaps soon.

I can accept my brokenness for the time. Yet I will hope and believe in my journey to wholeness.

Keeping Their Spirit Alive in Our Families

"My grandmother had a tremendous positive influence in my life. Even after she died, her spirit remained with me. During the birth of my daughter I knew that Grandma was close by my side; we named Chelsea Maria after her. I'm convinced that her gifts will always be carried on through my daughter. And Chelsea will always know her great grandmother, as we keep her memory alive."

Cindy Leines, in loving memory of her grandmother, Maria Erickson.

Many of us may wish to carry our loved one with us in spirit. We may choose to do this at family times and special events like reunions, weddings, births, funerals, and holidays. We may seek ways to bring their memory and presence into our family's lives by passing on their names, like Cindy did, by carrying on certain traditions, or by sharing their special sayings and keepsakes with others.

I will remind myself of the ways I keep my loved one's spirit alive in our family, especially during special times. I can honor their memory by passing on their traditions, sayings, and keepsakes.

Coming Out Of Grief

"Just beyond my window, the first fresh shoots of spring are slowly exposing themselves to the world. This gently signals to me that I can reenter the world as well."
Juliana Ehrman, in memory of her grandparents.

It may take a long time before we feel ready to fully enter the world again. Thus far, our shroud of grief may have kept us secluded and sheltered, and we may not have dared to venture far. Yet we can see new life all around us. It is ours to receive, if we just open our hearts and spirits to it.

It may be time to move on. Life is beckoning. We may need to summon the courage to live again.

I can come out of my shroud of grief and come closer to entering life fully again. Today I will take a walk, short or long, and breathe deeply of the world around me.

Acknowledging and Celebrating Their Life

"My beautiful son who didn't even have a chance to experience life's joys is gone! I cannot let his precious life go unnoticed. I will reach out to others who have lost loved ones in memory of him. I will let them know it's okay to take time to grieve this tremendous loss, and that others care and share in their grief. Though my son only lived for three short days, he changed my life forever."
Donna Roehl, "I love you, Andy."

No matter how long or short a life, our loved one's presence had an impact on this world. Acknowledging and celebrating their life is important and necessary, helping us to move on and heal. There are many ways to give tribute to them. Like Donna, we can offer compassion and understanding to others. We can encourage others to share their stories and support their feelings—whether they are sadness, confusion, or anger. We can be their companion as they struggle to accept reality.

Yes, death changes us forever. Remembering our loved one and sharing the bitter lessons of their death can help us make something positive out of our suffering.

I will give tribute to my loved one's life by offering compassion and understanding to others who need it.

Love Intensifies in Grief

"I have come a long way in my journey through grief. I will always long to hold my babies, and I will love them forever. What little memories I do have will always be with me. For you see, even in death, they have taught me how much a parent can love her children."

Dawn Fern, in memory of her children who died, Nichol Michele and Aaron Michael.

Our loved one's life and death may have touched us in special ways. Like Dawn, our love for them or for other special people has intensified.

Living without our loved one is hard to bear. Our emotions spring to the surface, reminding us what is important in our lives. We value the giving and receiving of love; beautiful gifts that have been magnified because of them.

I cherish all the memories and special feelings I have. I am ever thankful for my loved one's life.

We Never Stop Loving Them

"The best advice anyone ever gave me was to remember that I never have to stop loving her."

Elizabeth Levang, dedicated to her grandmother, Salute Belluz.

In the years that follow our loved one's death we may feel pressured to forget them and put them out of our minds. We may take this to mean that we should stop loving them, yet what we need to do is the exact opposite. Instead, we need to tell ourselves that we can love them forever, that it is our right, our gift to them and to ourselves. This thought can free us by allowing our hearts to remember them with love for the rest of our lives.

Though there are days when I can accept that my loved one died, I never have to forget them. I can love them always.

Nostalgic Moments

"It's good to remember my brother, and I'm glad I do. It means he hasn't gone away; he is still here. He will always be here, fitting me with shoes three sizes too big, insisting that I be on his team. Damn, it's good to be his brother! It always has been good. It always will be."
Mark D. Rittmann, "I miss you, Roger."

Memories of our loved one can often unleash a flood of nostalgia. Our heart can grow wistful as we think about the dreams and special bond we shared. We long to be with them again. We miss them. We want to recapture our past and once again delight in their presence.

Regretfully, we cannot turn back the hands of time. Only our memories and feelings of nostalgia will return us to yesterday. Even so, our longing reminds us that our loved one is close at hand.

The feelings of nostalgia that come over me bring my loved one close. My longing is a sign of loving.

Feeling We Will Never Get Over It

"It has been nearly two years since my aunt, my very special friend, died. I have struggled desperately to cope with the pain, which never leaves me. Well-wishers who think I have grieved long enough will have to wait a little longer. Grief is a very personal agony and must be dealt with individually."

　　　Anonymous

Grieving is a process which often lasts far longer than many people think it should. While we may be given messages that we should be "over it" by now, our heart reminds us we will never be over it, not really. We will always be affected by our loved one's life and death, their gifts, the impressions they made on us, and our loss. We may learn to live without them in a sense, but at the same time we learn to keep their spirit within us. This is the ultimate tribute to them, and the greatest gift from them.

I will free myself from the message that I must be over my grief by a specific time. I can trust that our love for each other will keep us entwined over time.

Drawing Strength

"My child was my guide in helping me grow even stronger in my relationship with my husband, with other people, and with myself. I found and still find that I have even more patience with children and adults, and I care about life even more. So even though my child never got the chance to grow physically, in my heart and emotions my child is a giant, and a large part of my life."

Lois Holmes, in loving memory of Baby Holmes.

Many of us are able to draw strength from our loved one, and, inspired by their memory, we make significant changes in our lives. From our pain and anguish we may decide to try to live more productive and meaningful lives. We may come to see the importance of family and friends, and work to establish closer relationships. Or, we may strive to understand ourselves better. Our loved one's death has helped us see life differently. The changes we make in our lives are their precious legacy.

The death of my loved one has changed me. I can draw strength from the legacy of love they have left me. I am thankful for this gift.

Acknowledging Our Long Struggle

"Paul and I have learned much from our precious little son. We have learned what real love is about. We have learned, too, that courage and strength can grow as far as we are willing to allow them, and that the human spirit has no limit."

> *Cathy Gunning, in loving memory of her son, Freddy.*

Surviving the death of our loved one is a mammoth struggle. Our suffering is long and agonizing. At times we may doubt that it will ever end. Yet as we heal, we may be fortunate to experience many triumphs of the heart. We may come to truly understand what love is, what life is all about, and what the human spirit is capable of enduring.

In many ways, grief brutally tests and challenges us. Still, we may find victories and successes to celebrate, and wisdom to be gained. It is important that we acknowledge the difficulties of our struggle and appreciate the new truths we have learned about ourselves.

I have shown great courage and strength as I have struggled to survive the death of my loved one. I am grateful for all that I have learned and achieved. I will celebrate my victories and successes.

Healing Over Time

"Judy's death remains a very real part of my life. For many years, I couldn't imagine how anything good could come from a tragedy so awful. But friends, support, love, and, yes, time, have brought new, worthwhile, even exciting reasons for life to go on."

Andrea Gambill, in loving memory of her daughter, Judy.

By now we can probably scarcely count how often we were told that time would heal our wounds. For a long while we may have thought these words were cruel and insensitive. All we had was time. Time to feel sad, angry, lonely, or crazy. Time to think about all we would never have, share, or experience. Time to remember and relive our loved one's life and death. Yet now we may feel we can admit that time has helped. It may have brought us peace, a sense of healing, and reasons to go on living.

The passage of time has made a difference. We can be grateful for what we have put behind us and for how far we have come.

There is no getting over my loved one's death, but I am making it through. I am grateful for all the healing time has brought.

Their Lasting Presence

"When my mother died, she left behind the most beautiful African Violets. I've been caring for them ever since, watering and feeding them. Like so many things, they have become a tangible extension of my mother. When they blossomed recently, it seemed like she was back with me again."

> Leah Jones, in loving memory of her mother, Ruth.

Months or years after a loss, there are still those times when we strongly sense the presence of our loved one. Is it intuition, or simply our mind tricking us? We may not be sure. Yet from time to time, many of us continue to feel a sudden and powerful closeness to our loved one. It doesn't matter where these feelings come from; we can be happy for the reminder, for the feeling of being close once again.

I can savor and enjoy those times when I sense my loved one is near. I can revel once again in our closeness.

Lingering "Whys"

"I'm still trying to deal with the 'whys.' My daughter's cardiologist explained to me that they were able to learn from what happened to her and have been able to help three other babies. I'm glad that something positive can come from it, but why did it have to be my daughter's death that helped them learn something? I know that someone else's baby would have died, and I don't wish that on anyone, but why did it have to be my Robin?"

Diane Crater, in loving memory of Robin Marie Crater, who died following surgery to correct a congenital heart defect.

Even after much time has passed, the "whys" may linger for many of us. We may still be searching, trying to find some logic to our loved one's death. Though we may appreciate that some good has come, it doesn't erase the questions or our sense of unfairness over it all. It is a lonely feeling to not know why.

Accepting what has happened can be an ongoing struggle, and trying to understand the "whys" is a natural part of this process. For now, it may be best to let the "whys" come and to share our confusion and frustration with a good listener.

I can search for answers if I choose. My questioning is a way to foster healing.

The Emotions and Memories
Unlocked by Music

"Whenever I hear the hymn 'Amazing Grace,' my heart fills with tears for my father. As each verse is sung, that weight in my heart increases. His memory becomes very strong, and with it I have the reassurance and comfort that he is now part of God's grace. I love you, Dad. 'How sweet the sound.'"

Karl Dedolph III, in memory of his father, Karl Dedolph, Jr.

Music, especially uplifting songs like 'Amazing Grace,' can have a profound affect on us in the months and years following our loved one's death. As this music fills our senses, we may find comfort in the sad and joyful memories that spring from our heart.

I can allow myself to experience the moods and memories that flow from me when inspirational music is played or sung.

Afterthoughts of the Heart
by Joyce Lung and Linda Moxley,
in loving memory of Ann Marie Cavnar.

Death claimed you not so long ago
And our sorrow is profound.
We still expect to see you...
Your presence is all around.

We cry for all the moments
We know will never be.
Now our memories must sustain us
As your spirit is set free.

We'll save your earthly treasures
That bring you back to mind.
The scent of you still lingers there
So you're not hard to find.

The family tree still bears your name
In the Bible handed through the years.
With love you'll always be remembered
As we shed bittersweet tears.

You will not be forgotten
As generations pass by.
We'll keep your memory in our hearts...
We'll never let it die.

Special Days, Moments, and Concerns

~

ONE WEEK ANNIVERSARY OF DEATH

Just One More Time
by Mary Laing Kingston,
in loving memory of her mother.

I walk into Mom's room
  no one to cover, no breaths to hear, no one to gather
in.
She is gone—one week, one week today.
  I sit in the dark in the chair
  where I sat those many nights.
  The clock ticks breaking the silence.

I remember looking into her brown eyes
  They were the eyes of my youth that held all life's
answers
  but they became the eyes that held in the suffering
  so they could twinkle with a laugh.

I remember looking into them when she started to say goodbye
   "Dying would be okay," she said,
   "If I knew you'd be alright."

"It's almost time, but I need to know—will you be alright?"

I couldn't see those brown eyes when I answered
  for my own were filled with tears.

And now she's gone.

So, here I sit alone in the dark
  wanting to see her just one more time—
  Just one more cup of coffee
  Just one more laugh
  Just one more hug
  Just one more goodbye.

My tears come freely now, thawed by the finality.
It is a relief to have them come now
 I held them so tightly for so long.
But in the dark, in her room, they come.
  Washing over me in the pain of knowing
  there won't ever be
  One more time.

ANNIVERSARY OF DEATH

Thoughts on an Anniversary
by Janis Heil, in memory of Jessica.

It's true that she's always in
the back of my mind.
But she's not always on my mind.

When I think of her now, I
remember her warmly.
I rarely cry anymore out of
hurt or anger.

But there are times when something
can throw me right back to that
very day.
And the depth of my feelings of
loss and pain once again equal
the depth of my love for her.

And I cry. And I hurt.
But it reminds me all the more
that she will always be
part of my life, and that she's
special enough to care about.

Time has healed me.
But time has not made me forget.

THE SEASON OF SPRING

April Showers

by Kathryn R. Power
"To Tony, my soulmate and friend."

Tears,
Tales,
Trials,
Troubles
Trails—endlessly marked out around
      the pond, to the marsh.
      Mother Earth wept with me.
This April cried, and showered my May with flowers.
 I am April rain.
 All the tears of April are mine,
        Thundering,
        Bolting, and
        Gently falling
        To Earth.

I am May
A flower unfolding—
A field of dandelions swaying
 To the wind's music.
May Day! A cry for life, rebirth,
 Me—a May flower
 Showered with possibilities for
      life after death.

Mother's Day

by Patti Fochi, in memory of her son, Justin.

A day to celebrate motherhood
               and I do celebrate
My two daughters fill my world with joy
I rejoice in their beings, their growth
Yet...
    there is a sadness
               an emptiness
A place in this mother's heart
   for the son, not living
An emptiness, never filled
   a quiet reserved place
An emptiness...

FATHER'S DAY

by Jim Nelson, in loving memory of David.

Sunday is Father's Day, and I feel awkward about it.
On a cold morning in January, our son, David, was born,
and I became a father.
Before that cold day ended our son was dead.
Was I a father still?

I had dreams for him,
hopes for him,
love for him, as any father would.
I grieved for him, longed for him,
missed him achingly
as only a father could.
Did the grieving and the longing and the missing
achingly
make me a father still,
though I no longer had the relationship or the function?

Father's Day is coming...
I am feeling confused and awkward about it.

Today is Sunday. Father's Day.
A friend appproaches me and says,
"Today must be terribly hard for you."
Then he gives me a hug, a heartfelt embrace, and says,
"I'll be thinking of you today. Happy Father's Day."

Suddenly, the awkwardness and confusion is gone.
I am a father.
I will always be one.

BIRTHDAY

Happy Birthday

*by Sherokee Ilse, in loving memory
of her grandmother, Genevieve Kriesch.*

It is your birthday today.
Happy Birthday!
Can't help but think of you,
Wishing we could talk, laugh, play
And remember together.
We would sing "Happy Birthday" to you,
Watch you blow out candles and make a wish.
We might talk of your birth, the past
And dreams of tomorrow.

Instead I shed tears as I smile,
Thinking of the gifts your life
Has given me, our family
And so many others.

Happy Birthday! We miss you.

LIFE CHANGES

The Nevers

*by Elizabeth Levang, in memory of
her uncle, Tony Rizzo.*

As I gather my baby close in my arms
We rock and sing our nighttime songs.
In the peace that comes with this calming time
I think of you.
And, I cry.

I cry for my precious daughter.
She will not know you.
She will never hear you call her name
Never smell the thick scent of your cigar
Never touch your rough and calloused hands
Never know your genuine love.

I cry for you.
You will not know my baby.
You will never welcome her into this world
Never watch her smile and sing
Never perch her on your knee
Never kiss her gently.

My baby's eyes are filled with sleep
The once still air is now sweetened by my tears.
In the quiet of this tender night
I think of you.
And, I cry.

SPECIAL CARE FOR GRIEVING CHILDREN

Comfort the Child
by Maria Frick

The tears fall
Silence prevails.
   confusion...
      unanswered questions,
         guilt,
            fear.
   Death has left its mark.
Incomprehendable
Especially for a child.

The child's words may not come so easy
Their pain...not so clearly understood
Still they struggle to grasp
Thoughts reflected by the heart.

Offer comfort,
   reassurance
      and a warm embrace.
Listen with a heart, not just an ear.

For
   the child's grief
      is as real as ours
As deep and painful.

With our love they will find hope
   strength
      peace
And, as the sun sets,
   Their tears and fearfulness will find retreat.

THE UNREALISTIC EXPECTATIONS
OF OTHERS

Damn Right I'm Bitter!
Damn Right I'm Angry!
by Mary Van Bockern, whose daughter,
Catie, died at age three.

I heard through the grapevine that
  you think I'm bitter.
  Damn right I'm bitter!
I heard that you wonder if I'm not
  "stuck" in the angry stage of grief.
Damn right I'm angry!
It's only been a few months; who gave you
  the right to decide how long I should grieve?

My beautiful daughter is dead.
Not out on a visit to grandma's.
Not off to school for the day.
dead.

I didn't pick out her Easter outfit with
  the intention of burying her in it.
I didn't bathe her little body and brush
  her hair knowing it was to be my last
  chance to touch her warmth, never imagining
  the next touch would be of a cold, hard,
  unmoving little girl.

Damn right I'm bitter!
Damn right I'm angry!

You have no right to judge me.
Believe me, you have no idea
  of what I'm trying to live through.

If I make you uncomfortable, believe me, you
    return the feeling.
You go home to your healthy, living children
    and wonder how I can act this way?

You go home to your normal life, while I
    go home to face a life without my daughter.
The rug has been jerked out from under me.
My network of faith, of religion seems to have
collapsed under me, with no safety net.
I am tumbling in a foreign life, grasping
    for something that will help this make sense.

You leave our meeting, rushing to take your
    children from the nursery to playschool.
You talk about the hassle of finding time to
    get your kids' Christmas outfits bought,
        their Christmas pictures taken, the expense of gifts.
I leave empty-armed, no hassles for me,
    except to return to my quiet empty home...alone.
No gift expenses for me, except funeral and the
    purchase of a plot of ground to place my baby in.
No big Christmas outfit decisions, only decisions
    for a headstone that is supposed to express our
    love for our dead daughter.

So...you think I'm bitter?
You think I'm angry?
Damn right I'm bitter!
Damn right I'm angry!

Who better?

FAMILY GATHERINGS

Longing For Him Still

*by Mary Connell, in memory of
her brother-in-law, Ken Connell.*

Husband.
Father.
Brother.
Uncle.
Son.
One person is gone.
But when we gather as a family for...
    a wedding,
    Thanksgiving dinner,
    fireworks on the Fourth of July,
I see all the roles you played for us
    and the unique loss each one of us feels.
The aching grief has given way with time
    to subtler forms of longing.
We reminisce, and laugh, and yet still mourn.
You were many different things to all of us
But, we all called you "friend."
Thanks be to God and His promise
    because of Christ we will meet again in glory.

ROSH HASHANAH AND YOM KIPPUR

A Letter to Our Son
by Estee and Howard Warsett

We miss you on your birthday,
Each Rosh Hashanah.
This time of reflection
And family togetherness
Rekindles our dreams and hopes for you.

Such dreams and plans,
Rich and beautiful,
Yet not to be fulfilled.
For on this day God chose you,
That you would be with Him.

Your innocence so divine.
Your soul so pure,
You need not be cleansed
On the High Holy Day of Yom Kippur.

In the little time we had with you,
A great lesson we were taught
—how fragile life really is
And how quickly it is lost.

Each holiday we think of you
At this special family time.
You are entwined within our hearts.
And we'll never say goodbye.

We love you, Baruch, our forever baby.

THE SEASON OF WINTER

Winter
by Roberta Hermansen

This winter's desolation is my desolation,
   It's barrenness, my heart.
      Some say spring will come,
         Trees will leaf,
            Buds will swell,
               New life will emerge.

But I feel winter in my heart,
   In my soul,
      In my being.
         I wonder if the ice will ever thaw
           So I can drink from it again
              To nourish my spirit.

CHRISTMAS

A Poem To My Son
by Ann Janni

Christmas has come and gone,
And still you were not here.
With every package that I wrapped,
I shed a silent tear.

How I longed for days gone by,
To have you by my side;
To watch you trim the Christmas tree
And see you smile with pride.

There were no lights at our house
The decorations, few.
For no one wanted to do the job
That once belonged to you.

The Christmas shopping I did alone
I missed your help there, too.
I baked the Christmas cookies
And my thoughts remained with you.

I signed the Christmas cards we sent
With love and tender care.
The thing that really hurt the most
Was that your name was not there.

We made our Christmas visits,
I smiled and tried to hide
All the pain and sorrow
That I have deep inside.

No one seems to understand,
I live from day to day.
And if I live a hundred years,
The pain won't go away!

THE NEW YEAR
by sascha

Old year has gone away
   With gift and candle —
   Old year has gone away
   With thought and song.
   Old year has given light
   And dark and season.
   Old year has been too short
   And been too long.

Old year has given joy
And disappointment.
Old year has given grief
And strength to cope.
Old year was memory
And was forgetting —
   Another year is come:
   Give it your hope.

Resources

The following organizations offer helpful information, referrals, and other resources.

AARP Grief and Loss Services
601 E St. NW
Washington, DC 20049
202-434-2260; www.aarp.org/griefandloss

American Association of Suicidology
4201 Connecticut Ave. NW, Suite 310
Washington, DC 20008
202-237-2280

The Compassionate Friends, TCF, National Office
PO Box 3696
Oak Brook, IL 60522-3696
630-990-0010; www.compassionatefriends.com

Mothers Against Drunk Driving (M.A.D.D.)
511 E. John Carpenter Freeway, Suite 700
Irving, TX 75062
800-438-MADD; www.madd.org

National AIDS Hotline
800-342-2437

National Cancer Institute
9000 Rockville Pike
Bethesda, MD 20892
800-422-6237; www.nci.nih.gov

National Institute of Mental Health—Public Inquiries
NIH—Neuroscience Center, Rm. 8184
6001 Executive Blvd., MSC 9663
Bethesda, MD 20892-9003
301-443-4513; www.nimh.nih.gov

The Pregnancy and Infant Loss Center
1421 E. Wayzata Blvd., Suite 70
Wayzata, MN 55391
612-473-9372

Elizabeth Levang, Ph.D., holds a doctorate in Human and Organizational Systems from the Fielding Institute in Santa Barbara, California. She has conducted many educational programs on grieving, has led several support groups, and is a consultant, speaker, and writer in the fields of human development and psychology. Her deep understanding of bereavement, from both academic and personal standpoints, inspired her to co-author *Remembering With Love*.

Sherokee Ilse is the author of *Empty Arms* and co-author of *The Anguish of Loss* and *Miscarriage: A Shattered Dream*. For over ten years she has conducted seminars on the subjects of grief and infant loss. The founder of The Pregnancy and Infant Loss Center, a national nonprofit organization, she also brings insight gained from personal grieving experiences to *Remembering With Love*.

Both authors live in Minneapolis, Minnesota.